Railway Memories No. 31

# RETFORD, WORKSOP & SHERWOOD FOREST

Written and compiled by Stephen Chapman

".....Here is a good market town - of the name of Worksop, where are the ruins of a monastery to be seen in the meadows on the east side of it, and the west end of the church, which is still standing, has two beautiful and fair towers. This place is noted for liquorice and malt."
*Daniel Defoe*

**BELLCODE BOOKS**
Church View, Middle Street
Rudston, East Yorkshire YO25 4UF
email: bellcode4books@yahoo.co.uk

Copyright © 2021 Bellcode Books
ISBN 9781871233 35 3

All rights reserved. The contents of this book are the copyright of Bellcode Books and their contributors and may not be reproduced in any form or posted on any internet website without the prior written consent of the copyright holder.

Designed and edited by Stephen Chapman

Printed in the UK by The Amadeus Press, Cleckheaton, West Yorkshire.

**ABOVE: In the early 1960s a WD 2-8-0 awaits its turn while Langwith Junction's O4 2-8-0 No. 63615 starts a train out of the Up yard at Mansfield Concentration Sidings, Clipstone.** *Tom Greaves*
**FRONT COVER: Local people turn out to mingle with visiting gricers at Shirebrook North station on 18th April 1964 as celebrated LNER A3 Pacific No.4472** *Flying Scotsman* **calls with the the Great Central Railtour.** *Stephen Chapman archive*
**BACK COVER TOP: It's coming up to 4pm one day in June 1958 and the Liverpool Central to Harwich Town boat train is calling at Worksop under the charge of B17/1 4-6-0 No. 61621** *Hatfield House. Geoff Warnes/Colour-Rail*
**BACK COVER BOTTOM: The Lancashire, Derbyshire & East Coast Railway had these big 0-6-4 tank engines for its coal runs to Grimsby. Under the LNER they were classed M1 and this Sail & Steam picture shows No. 6153 alongside Tuxford Works in the 1930s.** *Stephen Chapman archive*
**FRONTISPIECE: B17/6 4-6-0 No. 61657** *Doncaster Rovers* **rattles the Harwich Parkeston Quay to Liverpool boat train over the East Coast main line at Retford's flat crossing in the 1950s.** *John Foreman/Neville Stead collection/Transport Library*

# INTRODUCTION

With tales of Robin Hood, Maid Marian, the Sheriff of Nottingham and Sherwood Forest manifest today in endless orderly rows of plantation trees - these Dukeries - so named because of all the stately homes in the area - are a land of history and legends. It is a land where coal mining on the largest scale was supplanted on a rolling landscape of country estates, forests, farms and villages. And without doubt, this background has served to heighten the fascination of the railways that served this part of the East Midlands, where single tracks branched off the principal routes and meandered through field and forest to a galaxy of collieries.

But there was more to the railways of Sherwood than the day-in-day out business of shifting huge loads of coal and the grudging slow and spartan services that passengers on most lines had to be content with. There were express and long-distance freights - the nightly fish trains from Hull and Grimsby of the highest priority, while on summer Saturdays any goods line signalled for use by passenger trains would come alive with a succession of holiday expresses and excursions to the east coast resorts.

Back in steam days, Shirebrook was better known to those with a railway interest for Langwith Junction steam loco shed. In the 1960s when the new Shirebrook diesel depot opened, despite it being a relatively small depot, it quickly became a railway centre of some importance, being the force behind the continuous movement of coal throughout the locality. Worksop, with its extensive sidings was an important centre for coal movements and would ultimately come to be at the heart of railway operations. Retford, it's fair to say, has been somewhat unjustifiably downplayed as a railway centre. Situated on the intersection between the East Coast main line and an important cross-country route, with two motive power depots, and a wagon works not far away at Ranskill, not to mention being a calling point for East Coast expresses - and, as will be seen, a good location for photography - it was more significant than has been generally appreciated - by enthusiasts at any rate. However, since details of the famous expresses that have historically graced the busy and supremely important ECML have been aired over and over again by many publications over many years, this book focuses simply on enjoying the wonderful pictures of Retford contained within. Tuxford, again on an intersection with the East Coast main line, was the beating heart of the Lancashire, Derbyshire &East Coast Railway with its loco sheds, the company's workshops, and the twin level intersection station at Dukeries Junction.

## Contents

| | |
|---|---|
| Page 4 | The railways come to Sherwood |
| Page 19 | Retford G.N. |
| Page 33 | Retford - Woodhouse |
| Page 53 | Tuxford-Langwith Jn.-Killamarsh |
| Page 82 | The Mansfield Railway |
| Page 91 | Shireoaks - Mansfield |
| Page 110 | Pleasley and Teversal |
| Page 112 | Running late for Chesterfield |

Although this book is not specifically intended to be about Mansfield, we just have to briefly visit the metropolis at the heart of the coalfield which from 1964 was England's biggest town without a passenger service until the situation was happily rectified in the 1990s. Even in the third decade of 21st century when the Sprinter units that link Worksop with Nottingham, Sheffield, Retford and Lincoln are just about the only trains to be seen following the total annihilation of the coal industry that generated so much freight traffic, those lines that remain still retain something of their special character. So dramatic and comprehensive have been the changes in recent years that even 21st century scenes with class 66 locomotives qualify as railway memories.

In order to be concise, the area covered by this book will be referred to as Sherwood throughout. Wherever place names have more than one spelling, the version used in official railway documents is the one generally used. British Railways Sectional Appendix supplements may be quoted herein as the date for various changes to signalling etc. but it should be noted that the actual change may have taken place before the supplement was issued. On 7th September 1964 BR began using the 24-hour clock in its working timetables so we use am/pm up to that date and the 24-hour clock thereafter.

**The publisher's thanks are due** to all those who have provided material for this edition of Railway Memories. Also to Robert Anderson, Adrian Booth and Ron Hollier for their assistance. **Sources:** BR. LNER and LMS documents, working timetables, appendices, notices, press releases and publicity publications; Clinker's Register of Closed Lines and Stations; Durham Mining Museum; Graces's Guide; Industrial Railway Society; LNER List of Lines; Official Handbook of Stations 1938 and 1956, The Railway Clearing House; The Ordnance Survey; A Regional History of Railways, The East Midlands, Robin Leleux, David & Charles; A Regional History of Railways. South and West Yorkshire, David Joy, David & Charles; Signalling Atlas and Signal Box Directory of Great Britain and Ireland by Peter Kay; The Study Library.net.; contemporary editions of Modern Railways, Railway Magazine, The Railway Observer, Railway World and Trains Illustrated. **Tribute is especially paid** to all those photographers, named and unknown, for their foresight in recording what at the time may have been a mundane scene but which today are treasured images of a bygone age.

**IMPORTANT: Bellcode Books is not in a position to supply or locate copies of photographs reproduced in this book. Photographs and downloads can be purchased from some of the agencies credited in the picture captions.**

# The railways come to Sherwood

When it comes to deciding the birthplace of rail transport, the East Midlands has to be a serious contender, for way back in 1604, in the reign of the new King James, pamphletist William Gray reported that coal mining pioneer Huntingdon Beaumont had laid a two-mile wooden waggonway from his coal pits near Wollaton, just west of Nottingham. By 1819 Mansfield had a railway of sorts when a waggonway deploying bullock carts on angle iron rails was completed. At that time coal was mined in shallow pits to the west, in the Erewash and Rother valleys, the seams beneath Sherwood were far too deep to reach, and this Mansfield & Pinxton Railway was built to bring coal into Mansfield from the Erewash Valley via the Cromford Canal. The Sherwood Forest and Dukeries region was mainly agricultural with quarrying for limestone, building sandstone, sand and clay the main industries. The growing of barley led to the establishment of maltings at such places as Retford, Worksop and Langwith.

In spite of these early developments, some of Sherwood's railways did not open until the 1890s or even well into the 20th century and it is quite remarkable to recall that the last new line was built in the 1960s when railways all over the country were being closed. The first main line to appear on the scene was the Sheffield & Lincolnshire Junction Railway opened in July 1849. At Sheffield it connected with the Sheffield, Ashton & Manchester Railway - the Woodhead line - and at Gainsborough with the Great Grimsby & Sheffield Junction Railway, completing a direct cross-Pennine route all the way from Manchester to Grimsby. Before the line was completed the three constituents were merged into one company, the Manchester, Sheffield & Lincolnshire Railway which would rename itself the Great Central Railway upon completion of its main line to London in 1899. The main aim of the line's promoters was to connect the forges of Sheffield with the sea at Grimsby but before long it would also find lucrative business in transporting the ingredients of a new convenience food for the hungry masses of the West Riding and Lancashire industrial towns - North Sea fish and Lincolnshire potatoes for chips. On the way it served Worksop and Retford which were small market towns then. At Gainsborough it connected with the Great Northern Railway to Lincoln, Boston and Peterborough. Less than three months later, on 9th October the Midland Railway reached Mansfield when it opened its line from Nottingham, having taken over and upgraded the Mansfield & Pinxton in the process.

Retford was established as a railway junction in summer 1852 when the Great Northern Railway completed the final section of the present East Coast main line through the town.

**A 1950s scene from Retford's Thrumpton Lane level crossing footbridge showing the remains of the town's first station, opened in 1849 by the Manchester, Sheffield & Lincolnshire Railway and closed to passengers in July 1859 when MS&L trains began using the present day Great Northern station. The goods facilities seen beyond the station buildings survived until December 1970, latterly downgraded to an unstaffed public delivery siding and renamed Thrumpton since 1924. In the left background can be seen the malthouses, a notable line of business in Retford.** *Railway Station Photographs*

A3 Pacific No. 60050 *Persimmon* thunders through the Great Northern station at Retford with a Bradford/Leeds-Kings Cross post-Easter relief express at 4.15pm on Wednesday 20th April 1960. From 1859 MS&L line trains also used this station until completion of the underpass in 1965 and installation of low level platforms on the MS&L line. Since then only a handful of Sheffield and Worksop trains have used this station which remains as important as ever although much has changed. The platform face on the left has been eliminated with all Down calling trains using the island face on the far left. The line has been electrified and the station buildings on the left long since replaced by simpler, modern constructions but those on the right remain much the same. *Robert Anderson*

It crossed the MS&L by a flat crossing which would be a defining feature of the railway there. Seven years later, connecting curves were laid enabling MS&L trains to use the GN station.

By this time new deep mining techniques were developing fast and the coalfield was spreading eastwards in search of the deeper and richer seams; with it would come more railways. In 1866 the Midland completed a line from Tibshelf in the Erewash Valley to pits in the Butcherwood and Teversal area which it extended to Pleasley in 1877. In April 1871 it completed the line from Mansfield to Southwell beyond which the existing branch to Rolleston Junction connected with its Nottingham-Lincoln line. A crucial line opening took place in June 1875 when it extended its Nottingham-Mansfield line northwards to Shireoaks where it met the MS&L via a triangular junction allowing trains to turn both east and west. Along the way it served Steetley and Shireoaks collieries, the only pits open along the route at that time. By the 1890s, it would also serve big new mines at Sherwood, Shirebrook, Langwith, Creswell, and Whitwell. And so the Midland continued to spread its tentacles as it mopped up much of the coal traffic on offer from the newly emerging coalfield.

In May 1886 it completed a line going west from the Mansfield-Shireoaks line at Pleasley Junction, just north of Mansfield Woodhouse, to Pleasley where it met the line from Tibshelf. In 1888, after taking over and upgrading a number of colliery tramways the Midland opened the line from Elmton & Creswell to Clowne and Staveley, and two years later the line from Pleasley to Bolsover creating a second route to Staveley and Chesterfield. In September 1890 it introduced passenger services by both these routes.

The Midland had had things its own way so far but the 1890s saw it finally facing competition. The Great Northern Railway, wanting its share of coal traffic, entered the scene when it extended its Leen Valley line north from Kirkby-in-Ashfield(Kirkby South Junction) to Sutton-in-Ashfield in 1898 which it then took forward to Pleasley along with a branch from Skegby to Teversal in 1900. Although a station was provided at Teversal it saw no regular passenger service other than miners' trains. The following year the GN completed the through route to Langwith Junction where it met the Lancashire, Derbyshire & East Coast Railway, a young upstart company with big ideas.

The LD&EC planned a coast to coast main line linking Liverpool, Warrington, Manchester and Chesterfield with Lincoln and a new deep water port on the Lincolnshire coast at Sutton-on-Sea. Although it failed to attract backing for its ambitious cross-Pennine section or the port, the Chesterfield-Lincoln portion was built and completed by March 1897. This section had considerable support from the Great Eastern Railway which had its eyes on the industrial riches of South Yorkshire, Nottinghamshire and North Derbyshire, not to mention the movement of coal to

The 3.47pm Worksop to Nottingham service headed by Stanier Class 4 2-6-4T No. 42629 passes Shirebrook Junction and approaches Shirebook West station at 4.11pm on 13th October 1962. The trackbed of the spur up to Langwith Junction opened in 1904 is just visible beyond the last coach. *Robert Anderson*

London. It had already reached Lincoln via its joint line with the Great Northern, completed in 1882. From Langwith Junction the LD&EC, as it would be known to the present day, had already laid a branch to Barlborough Colliery (Clowne,) along with connections to the new Warsop, Creswell and Langwith collieries. It intersected the East Coast main line at Tuxford where a two-level interchange station with the Great Northern known as Dukeries Junction was established along with main workshops, a motive power depot and a north-facing curve down to the GN main line. It also established the engine shed at Langwith Junction. In 1898 the line from Clowne to Beighton Junction on the Midland's old Leeds-Derby main line in the Rother Valley was added, providing the LD&EC - and the Great Eastern - with access to Sheffield. Curves connecting it to the Midland at Shirebrook were installed from Warsop Junction(in 1899) and Langwith Junction(1904.) Despite its failure to attract interest in its western and eastern extremities, and despite what was built being gradually whittled away from each end, the LD&EC was destined to be the most remarkable of survivors. And, the deep water port was eventually built by its successor, the Great Central - not at Sutton but at Immingham which at the time of writing handles more rail tonnage than any other port in Britain, thus vindicating the grand vision held by the line's promoters.

By this time railway and coal extraction development in the area was coming to its peak and a complex local network was starting to emerge. But despite the presence of three different companies, coal owners and business leaders in Mansfield remained less than happy with the continuing dominance of the Midland Railway in their area, especially since they were developing big new deep mines at Blidworth, Rufford and Clipstone. Consequently they set up their own company, the Mansfield Railway which would join the new pits in the area to the LD&EC - which had been bought by the Great Central in 1907 - in the north and to the GC main line at Kirkby-in-Ashfield in the south. The first section was open for coal traffic from Mansfield (Crown Farm) Colliery to Kirkby South Junction by 1913. A branch was completed to Rufford Colliery when that came on stream and the section from Clipstone East Junction in 1916. Construction continued despite the First World War since coal supply was of the utmost importance.

The Midland wasn't going to be left behind, it had branches to Clipstone, Blidworth and Rufford collieries from its Southwell line. Clipstone Colliery, notable for its twin headstocks which have been preserved, came on stream in 1922, and Blidworth in 1926. Also opening at this time was Bilsthorpe Colliery in 1927, at the end of a $3_{1/2}$-mile branch from the Mansfield Railway's Blidworth and Rufford branch. Extensive sidings were established at Clipstone, officially known as Mansfield Concentration Sidings, where the coal traffic from all these new pits was brought together and remarshalled into trains for onward movement, and the returning empties sorted for distribution back to the collieries. Other railways had sidings at various key points: the LD&EC at Warsop, Boughton, Tuxford; the Midland at Shirebrook Colliery and Sherwood Colliery, and the GC at Retford, and at Worksop with extensive yards on both the Up and Down sides. Further south was the Midland yard at Kirkby-in-Ashfield.

By the 1920s, many collieries were being served by both the London & North Eastern Railway(the GC and Mansfield Railway's successor after the 1923 Grouping) and the London Midland & Scottish Railway(the Midland's successor.) Together they embarked on a new joint line, the Mid-Notts, from Hucknall, via Farnsfield on the Mansfield-Southwell line, and Ollerton, to a junction with the Sheffield-Retford line at Checker House in order to provide a more direct coal route to the port at Immingham. The Farnsworth-Bilsthorpe-Ollerton section was completed in 1930, providing the LMS with direct access to Bilsthorpe and Ollerton collieries, but economic depression and then the Second World War permanently halted construction on the other sections. Part of the route north of Ollerton was resurrected, however, for the final piece of railway to be built in Sherwood, the 4 1/2-mile branch completed in 1961 from Boughton, on the LD&EC, to the new Bevercotes mine which began producing coal in 1963. This branch required extensive civil engineering works - eleven bridges and a 250-yard tunnel to preserve farmland while half was in cuttings and the other half on embankments. And so, Sherwood's railways had reached their peak.

**Passenger services**

So far as passenger services are concerned Sherwood may be regarded as something of a railway backwater sandwiched between the East Coast main line to the east, and the Great Central and Midland main lines to the west, and it is true that many of the lines were mineral branches built primarily for coal. But the area has not been without some notable express passenger trains while on summer Saturdays, long after the passenger services on all but one line had been withdrawn, the railways came alive again with passengers.

**Sheffield-Retford:** During its time the Great Central's Sheffield-Worksop-Retford route has carried Manchester-Cleethorpes expresses, a Liverpool-Yarmouth and Lowestoft Through Corridor Express, a Manchester-Yarmouth Luncheon Corridor Express, the time-honoured, unofficially-titled North Country Continental Liverpool-Harwich boat train which ran this way until rerouted via Nottingham from May 1973, and a Leicester-Cleethorpes express which came off the GC main line via the Waleswood Curve. At various times in its history it has been an arm of the East Coast main line with King's Cross-Manchester expresses and even Pullman trains. In 1925 the

**Climbing away from Killamarsh Junction on the LD&EC line to Shirebrook North, O4 2-8-0 No. 63776 takes on the 1 in 100 gradient with a 1,000-ton load of empties, believed to be the 8.40am Greasborough Road(Rotherham)-Warsop Junction, at 11.50am on 24th November 1962.** *Robert Anderson*

LNER introduced a commercially unsuccessful and short-lived Kings Cross-Manchester Pullman. Undeterred by history British Railways, in September 1958, introduced two Sheffield-Kings Cross Pullmans each way, the Up morning train and Down evening train bearing The Master Cutler name transferred from the GC main line. So prestigious were they that even in 1958 diesel haulage was compulsory- even if a humble Brush Type 2(Class 31) was all that was available. They lasted 10 years before being withdrawn. In the 1960s, a second plan drawn up by then BR chairman Dr. Beeching - who needs no introduction - "Beeching 11" of 1965 advocated switching Sheffield-London services from St. Pancras to Kings Cross via Retford by 1984 - and as late as the 1980s, BR's newly-formed InterCity business sector considered the same idea. Even now, with open access operators and franchisees extending their tentacles, a return of London services over this line can never quite be ruled out(at least until the 2020/1 pandemic cast doubt over everything.) Class 1 expresses did in fact return to the route in 2019 with an hourly Northern Rail Leeds-Sheffield-Lincoln limited stop service, though the trains themselves appear little different to those operating the hourly Sheffield-Gainsborough Central stopping service which simultaneously replaced the previous Sheffield-Lincoln stopping service.

In summer 1959, the public timetable showed around 20 mid-week passenger trains each way a day through Worksop. The core of the service were five Sheffield Victoria-Cleethorpes trains, by then operated by Diesel Multiple Units(DMUs) with four from Cleethorpes, and five Sheffield-Lincoln trains each way, all but one being DMUs - the 3.40pm from Sheffield, booked to call at Worksop 4.18-19, and specified "Steam Train." In addition to the Sheffield-Cleethorpes DMUs were three Manchester London Road-Cleethorpes trains and a loco-hauled Sheffield-Cleethorpes express. One of the Manchester trains ran overnight conveying newspapers and calling at Worksop 3.35-4.0am. In the other direction only one Cleethorpes-Manchester train ran via this route. East of Retford, the Cleethorpes trains ran via Brigg and Barnetby while the Lincoln trains ran via Leverton, Cottam and Torksey until closure of that route in November 1959 when the service was rerouted via Gainsborough Lea Road. During the early 1990s the by then sparse Sheffield-Cleethorpes service of just three trains each way was proposed for replacement by buses which led to the term "bustitution" being coined. The rail service survived but by 1994 it was running only on Saturdays: at the time of writing the passenger service was suspended due to the pandemic.

The more important trains on the route in 1959 were of course the Sheffield Pullmans, the Harwich boat train and a Manchester Central-Cambridge service which ran Mondays, Fridays and Saturdays. The Pullmans became especially interesting for diesel fans - if there were any at that time. First they were hauled by the first of the English Electric Type 4s(class 40) but in the 1960s they became a test

**The diesel prototypes of the 1960s were frequently put to work on the Sheffield Pullmans. In this view, the Birmingham Railway Carriage & Wagon Co./Sulzer Type 4 D0260** *Lion* **calls at Retford with the afternoon Sheffield-King's Cross Pullman on Monday 30th April 1962.** *Peter Cookson*

run for new Type 4 prototypes and the Brush *Falcon*, Birmingham Sulzer *Lion* and English Electric DP2 all had turns on the Pullman. They passed Worksop non-stop but the Harwich boat train with its restaurant car did call there.

On summer Saturdays extra trains were laid on to cope with the mass movement of holidaymakers to and from the east coast resorts. With Skegness traditionally the most popular destination, three trains were advertised to run there in 1959, one starting from Sheffield Victoria, one from Manchester London Road, and the 7.10am from Tibshelf Town which ran via the GC main line and the Waleswood curve. It was not advertised to call at Worksop but was oddly shown to depart Woodhouse at 8.26. It seems that this was a timetable printing error and that the time should be Kiveton Bridge, shown on the line below. The return train, 1.47pm from Skegness, was shown to call at Kiveton Bridge at 4.9pm. There were also two trains to Yarmouth - one from Sheffield and one from Manchester Central - one from Manchester London Road to Cleethorpes, and one from Manchester Central to Sutton-on-Sea. One summer curiosity which ran every day was the 5.45am anglers' special from Wadsley Bridge(closed to regular passenger services since 15th June) to Woodhall Junction between Lincoln and Boston, and its return service. On Sundays there were four such trains to either Woodhall or Boston, including one from Rotherham.

**Worksop-Mansfield Town:** Besides the above, Worksop also had the service over the Midland line from Nottingham via Mansfield which was purely local in nature. The summer 1961 public timetable advertises, between 5.47am and 8.5pm, six Nottingham Midland-Worksop trains each way, plus one from Worksop to Mansfield Town and two from Mansfield to Worksop. There were also the 7.30am Elmton & Creswell to Nottingham and 4.40pm return to Whitwell. Judging by the timings and that the latter did not run on Saturdays, but with the absence of local knowledge, these appear very much like school trains. No doubt there will be those who have personal memories. Additional trains on Saturdays for nights out on the town were the 10.40pm Nottingham-Elmton & Creswell and 10.10pm Worksop-Mansfield.

Extra trains laid on for the summer holiday rush were the Friday nights 11.40pm Shirebrook West-Yarmouth and Saturday Only 12 noon return from Yarmouth, arriving Shirebrook West at 5.12pm, and the 7.15am Saturday Radford-Blackpool North and 10.50 from Blackpool return which ran via Seymour Junction and Clowne & Barlborough(see Railway Memories No.30 page 15.) More trains ran between Mansfield Town and Nottingham, including the Saturday Only 7.35am through carriages to St. Pancras. There was no Sunday service. The daily passenger service was withdrawn with effect from 12th October 1964 but reinstated in 1997/98 under the most ambitious railway reopening seen in Britain up to that point in time. Branded The Robin Hood Line, the new service required substantial engineering works which not only involved building new stations but reinstating abandoned lines and even building a new stretch of railway south of

Last day of Worksop-Nottingham passenger services. Stanier 2-6-4T No. 42588 of Nottingham shed calls at Mansfield Woodhouse with the 11.58 Nottingham-Worksop on 10th October 1964. *Tony Cooke//Colour Rail*

Kirkby-in-Ashfield where part of the line had been completely lifted and the earthworks destroyed, built over and even used for landfill, following abandonment of the original line.

The rest of Sherwood's railways carried what can best be described as skeleton services withdrawn before the 1960s, although most lines equipped to carry passenger trains continued to be used by summer Saturday and bank holiday extras to the east coast resorts along with many privately-charted trains - not least those organized by miners' welfare clubs.

**The LD&EC:** East of Langwith Junction the LD&EC - or "Clog and Knocker" as it was nicknamed but which the company promoted as "The Dukeries Line" - saw just two LNER Chesterfield Market Place to Lincoln trains a day in summer 1946(6th May to 6th October) and three from Lincoln. Three more trains ran from Chesterfield to Shirebrook North, one from Chesterfield to Mansfield Central, and one from Shirebrook North to Lincoln. In the other direction two more ran from Shirebrook North to Chesterfield and one from Mansfield to Chesterfield. There were also three trains each way between Edwinstowe, Mansfield Central and Nottingham Victoria. The LD&EC was well used by summer Saturday trains and in 1946 they included Chesterfield-Skegness, Kirkby-in-Ashfield-Skegness, Leicester-Cleethorpes and Leicester-Bridlington-Scarborough trains. There was no Sunday service.

The passenger service between Shirebrook North and Chesterfield was withdrawn from 3rd December 1951 upon complete closure of the line between Shirebrook North and just east of Duckmanton due to serious structural problems with Bolsover Tunnel, an event which also meant the line ceased to be a through route from the GC main line at Duckmanton Junction. The remainder of the daily service was axed with effect from 19th September1955 though the Nottingham-Mansfield-Edwinstowe trains continued until January 1956. Regular summer Saturday services continued until September 1964.

The passenger service on the LD&EC line from Langwith Junction to Beighton via Clowne South and Spink Hill was operated jointly by the Midland/LMS and GC/LNER and ran via the Langwith Junction-Shirebrook curve. In 1922 they ran three trains each way on weekdays between Mansfield(MR) and Sheffield(MR) plus one extra each way on Saturdays and a Saturday 10pm Langwith Junction-Clowne South. The service was withdrawn in 1939 but the line continued to be used for summer Saturday extras and some seasonal GC main line services, particularly overnight trains.

**Mansfield Central-Clipstone:** The former Mansfield Railway once had the glory of a daily London express, courtesy of the Great Central. In 1922 this was the 8.12am Mansfield Central to Marylebone Breakfast Car Express and the returning Restaurant Car Express due into Mansfield at 7.53pm. In those days there was a local weekday service operated by the GC of three Nottingham Victoria to Ollerton trains plus one from Nottingham to Edwinstowe, and four from Ollerton to Nottingham. More

**Langwith Junction-based A5 4-6-2T No. 69815 has charge of an LD&EC line passenger service at Shirebrook North in the early 1950s.**
*Neville Stead collection/Transport Library*

**Long after its regular passenger service had ceased, the LD&EC was a prime route for summer Saturday services to and from the east coast resorts. At 4.24pm on 26th August 1961, K3 2-6-0 No. 61953 of Colwick shed is seen approaching Edwinstowe with the 2.12pm Skegness-Basford North. The K3s and B1 4-6-0s were normal power for these services but from summer 1962 were mostly replaced by Type 2 and 3 diesels.** *David Holmes*

trains ran between Mansfield Central and Nottingham. By summer 1946 passenger trains between Mansfield Central and Clipstone consisted of Nottingham-Edwinstowe trains departing Mansfield at 7.4 and 10.1am and 7.15pm. Connections for Lincoln were available off the morning trains at Edwinstowe. Trains ran from Edwinstowe to Nottingham at 7.48am, 10.40am and 7.52pm from Edwinstowe. The service was withdrawn from 2nd January 1956 but Mansfield Central was still used for summer Saturday extras, the summer 1961 public timetable advertising trains to Skegness, Mablethorpe, Cleethorpes and Scarborough with corresponding return workings plus one each way between Ollerton and Yarmouth.

**Shirebrook North-Sutton-in-Ashfield.** Well into BR days some seasonal long distance expresses on the GC main line, especially at night, were routed between Nottingham and Sheffield via the Leen Valley Extension, Langwith Junction and Spink Hill. Back in 1922 the Great Northern ran a local service of four trains each way between Nottingham Victoria and Shirebrook South - extended by the LNER to Shirebrook North in 1925 - calling at Sutton-in-Ashfield, Skegby and Pleasley East; extras ran on Wednesdays and Saturdays. There was no Sunday service and the daily service was withdrawn in September 1931, but reinstated as far as Sutton-in-Ashfield in February 1956 and finally withdrawn in September 1956. Stations were retained for summer Saturday traffic and excursions until 1964, and the summer 1961 timetable advertised two Saturday Only trains each way - the 6am Shirebrook North-Nottingham with through carriages to Skegness and the 1.5pm Nottingham-Shirebrook North with through carriages from Skegness, plus the 1.25pm Shirebrook North-Nottingham and 5.25pm return. These trains called at Shirebrook South, Pleasley East, Sutton-in-Ashfield Town, Hucknall Central and Bulwell Common. There was no advertised service on any other day.

**Other Mansfield services:** The Midland also ran three trains each way between Mansfield, Pleasley, Bolsover and Chesterfield or Barrow Hill in 1922 plus two extras on Saturdays. It operated the same level of service between Mansfield and Chesterfield or Barrow Hill via Elmton & Creswell and Clowne & Barlborough. On the Mansfield-Southwell line it ran just two Mansfield-Newark trains each way per weekday(plus one extra on Saturday evenings,) calling at Blidworth & Rainworth, Farnsfield, Kirklington, Southwell and Rolleston Junction. There was no Sunday service on any of the lines mentioned in this paragraph.

Once bus competition made its mark these local services, which were often very slow, began to disappear. The Southwell service was withdrawn as early as August 1929, the Mansfield-Pleasley-Chesterfield service in 1930, the Mansfield-Sheffield Midland service soon after the outbreak of war, on 10th September 1939, while the the Mansfield-Chesterfield service via Elmton & Creswell had

**Here, L1 2-6-4T No. 67760 calls at Sutton-in-Ashfield with a 1950s Nottingham-Shirebrook North service. The absence of a shedplate suggests 67760 has just transferred to Colwick from its 1950s home at Neasden.** *Neville Stead collection/Transport Library*

dwindled to one train day by the time it was axed in July 1954. By the mid-1960s every line except Sheffield-Retford had lost its regular daily passenger service, and Mansfield was crowned with the dubious mantle of being England's biggest town without a regular passenger service.

**Freight**

Freight traffic was predominantly coal and the presence of modern highly productive collieries ensured the survival of most lines in whole or in part for freight right into the 21st century. Until the late 1960s most freight movements consisted of the humble, unglorious but vital class 8 trains of unbraked loose-coupled mineral wagons endlessly moving coal from the various pits, together with trains of returning empties which were usually class 7. The following review comes from the summer 1963 working timetable (17th June-8th September.)It is worth noting when considering the numbers of trains quoted that many did not run on Monday mornings or were retimed to run later while on summer Saturdays many were suspended to leave capacity and resources available for the heavy holiday passenger traffic of the time. It's fair to say that generally express freights ran at night while most mineral workings and trips were during the day. Of course, there were exceptions and it would be normal for trains to be cancelled or additional trains to run on the day. Many of the longer distance freights ran over the Pennines to Mottram sidings where wagons were remarshalled for their final destinations and in the east to Whitemoor marshalling yard(March) and New England(Peterborough) where they were similarly remarshalled.

**Woodhouse East-Retford:** Information available to the author does not extend to a complete survey of the Sheffield-Retford line but the section between Woodhouse East Junction and Shireoaks East Junction saw 30 plus booked freights each way per weekday 24 hours giving us a good idea of the level and type of traffic on this line. Unlike other lines in the area, less than half the freights on this route were class 8 mineral trains. In fact there was a great variety ranging from 3M39 the 5.13pm Grimsby-Ashton Moss fish train down to class 8 trips serving Brookhouse, Kiveton Park, Shireoaks and Manton Wood collieries. Nor did hardly any two trains run between the same origin and destination. The only real exceptions were four class 8 trains from Rotherwood to Frodingham conveying coke from the Orgreave plant to the Scunthorpe steel works, along with their returning empties. The only others were 10 westbound(Down)class 8s from Worksop - three to Sheffield Broughton Lane, two to Neepsend, two going over Woodhead to Mottram yard and one each to Sheffield Bernard Road, Orgreave and Penistone Barnsley Junction. In addition was the 12.45am Worksop-Mottram class 4(fitted throughout with continuous brake.) In the Up direction two class 8s were booked to run from Ickles (Rotherham) to Worksop. Otherwise, there were as many origins and destinations as there were trains. Perhaps the most important after the fish train, were arguably 4E80 the 11.35pm Bernard Road to King's Cross Goods - and the corresponding 9.5pm class 4 from King's Cross, both "Assured Arrival" services. Also of priority were 4M34, the 9.6pm Westwood-Manchester Ardwick, 4M36 12.30am Lincoln West Yard-Mottram, the 10.25pm class 7 Whitemoor-Broughton Lane and 7E65 the 12.12am Dewsnap-Lincoln Pyewipe which were also "Assured Arrival services." The line also saw class 4 trains running Grimsby Docks-Mottram, Whitemoor-Ordsall Lane (Salford,) Immingham-Glazebrook and return, Widnes-Thames Haven, Ancoats-Grimsby and Lincoln West Yard-Rotherwood. Class 5 express freights ran New England-Mottram, Bernard Road-New England, Bernard Road-Whitemoor, Ancoats-Whitemoor and there was the 11.20pm Greasborough Road(Rotherham)-Highdyke iron ore empties. There were also the Saturdays Only 3.15pm Grimsby East Marsh-Guide Bridge and 7.22pm Lincoln West Yard-Mottram. Going against the usual routine for early Monday mornings was a "flight" of three Monday Only class 5 trains from Dewsnap Yard(Guide Bridge): 5E62 the 1.42 am to Whitemoor, 5E64 the 2.15am to New England and 5E63 the 2.30am to Grimsby, due to pass Woodhouse Junction at 4.7, 3.57(held to let 5E62 pass) and 4.25 respectively. Class 6 partly fitted freights ran Immingham-Mottram, Grimsby West Marsh-Bernard Road, Bernard Road-Worksop, Dewsnap-New England, Widnes-Immingham and Dewsnap-Retford Low Yard. Around half a dozen booked trains a day travelled to and from the GC main line via the Waleswood curve. They were mainly Staveley or Annesley-Kiveton Park, Worksop, Frodingham, Grimsby and Immingham class 8s.

**The LD&EC:** In summer 1963 when diesel traction was really starting to take the place of steam, the LD&EC was indeed a busy freight line. Any traffic summary has to review it in two parts, west of Clipstone and east of Clipstone since a great many workings started and terminated at Mansfield Concentration sidings. Along with the Mansfield Railway south through Mansfield Central, this eastern portion of the LD&EC was also a key link in the GC trunk freight route between the Humber Ports and steel plants of Scunthorpe and the yards at Annesley, and at Woodford(Buckinghamshire) where lines to South Wales and the West left the GC London line.To the east between Clipstone and Tuxford were between 46 and 48 booked trains each way per weekday 24 hours. Most significant on this section were the heavy, mainly diesel-hauled, class 7 block coal trains for London from Mansfield Concentration Sidings to New England and Whitemoor yards via Lincoln and the GN&GE Joint line, as well as others running to Immingham. Seven a day to Whitemoor, five to New England and six to Immingham plus two from Warsop Junction sidings to Whitemoor. Seven trains of returning empties ran from each plus one each from New England and Whitemoor running class 4. Besides the many class 8

*A WD 2-8-0 plods out of the murk as it passes Worksop station with a Down(westbound) class 8 minerals in this bleak 1960s scene. In the mist beyond the train are the maltings which, as with Retford, were a significant part of the Worksop commercial scene.*
*Stephen Chapman archive*

coal and mineral trips to and from Thoresby and Ollerton pits(Bevercotes was yet to come fully on stream) and to places further afield such as Hull, Immingham, Lincoln, Boston, and from Ollerton to St. Swithin's Power Station(Lincoln,) were two Frodingham-Annesley steel trains with four class 8s the other way coming throughout from Woodford.

The line also had its fair share of express freight and top priority were the fish trains: 3V05 3.30pm Hull-Plymouth, 3V11 4.30pm Grimsby Docks-Whitland, 3V07 6.5pm Hull-Banbury and 6.25 New Clee-Banbury, just shown as class 3 because in reality it combined with 3V07 at Mansfield Concentration Sidings where they arrived at 8.38pm and 8.55 respectively. The combined train then departed at 9.7 going forward to join the Great Central main line. The 6E02 4.55am Annesley-Grimsby West Marsh was an "Assured Arrival" service. Class 4 fully fitted express freights, again mostly at night, took the LD&EC en-route from Whitemoor to Mottram, Stretford and Manchester Ducie Street, from Lincoln West Holmes to Annesley, and from Woodford to Grimsby Docks; class 5s from Dewsnap to Whitemoor, Woodford and Annesley to Doncaster Belmont and Woodford to New Clee; and class 6 partly fitted trains from Doncaster Bank and Immingham to Annesley. A class 8 pick-up ran throughout from Warsop to Lincoln serving stations and sidings on the way, while another ran the opposite way to Langwith Junction.

Between Clipstone and Warsop Junction the LD&EC carried 22 booked Down trains and just 17 booked Up trains at this time but there was also a large number of light engine and engine and brake van movements between Langwith Junction engine shed, or Shirebrook diesel depot, and Mansfield Concentration sidings. Other freights also worked between Warsop Junction and the Spink Hill line, and the Midland line via Shirebrook Sidings.

The through long-distance and express freights have already been mentioned above and most others were class 7 or 8 mineral trains. Of note were six class 8 coal trains each day that went from Mansfield Concentration Sidings to Mottram and two each from Welbeck and Thoresby Colliery junctions to Shirebrook Sidings. One ran from Warsop to Annesley, three from Welbeck and two from Bernard Road to Mansfield Concentration Sidings. Class 7 trains included one each from Dewsnap and Northwich to Mansfield Concentration Sidings, from Ollerton to Mottram, Mansfield Concentration Sidings to Warsop, and from Mansfield Concentration Sidings to Staveley.

GC main line express and long-distance freights routed via the Leen Valley Extension, Langwith Junction, Spink Hill and Killamarsh included the 3.40am 8N64 Woodford-

**The 9.20am Lincoln West Yard-Langwith Junction pick-up passes through Boughton Halt headed by 04/8 2-8-0 No. 63829 at 2.5pm on 13th March 1963. No. 63829 was originally one of those Robinson 2-8-0s supplied direct to the army's Railway Operating Division for First World War service, but had been rebuilt during the late 1950s with a B1 boiler.** *David Holmes*

*Doncaster-based 9F 2-10-0 No. 92201 drifts down from Spink Hill towards Killamarsh with oil tanks at 6.10pm on 26th May 1962.*
*Robert Anderson*

Tees, 7.35am 4N24 Woodford-York, 2.23pm 8N79 Woodford-Tees empties, 3.49pm 8E41 Woodford-Frodingham, 4N23 6.35pm Woodford-York, 8M80 9.55pm York Skelton New Sidings-Annesley, 8M50 3.55am Frodingham-Annesley, 8M09 10.20am York Skelton New Sidings-Annesley, 9.40pm 4M20 Dringhouses-Woodford, 8M65 8.5pm Hull-Annesley, and possibly the most important of all - 4N19 the 6.10pm Burton-York beer train. There was also the odd Bernard Road-Annesley class 5, Annesley-Worksop class 8. Annesley-Mottram class 8, and Colwick-Bernard Road class 7. On top of these of course were all those trains passing Clipstone to/from Sheffield and over the Pennines, as mentioned previously.

The line's bread and butter class 7 and 8 workings also included trains between Warsop Junction and a whole variety of origins and destinations on this and the other side of the Pennines. Examples include three class 8s from Warsop to Mottram, two to Bernard Road and three from Heaton Mersey. Class 8 trips serviced Langwith, Creswell and Westthorpe collieries. Three long distance coal trains started from Spink Hill, two running direct to Walton (Liverpool) and one to Partington(Cheshire.) All in all, around 30 booked trains each way per mid-week 24 hours. Even so, timings were such that certain times of the day could see gaps of over 90 minutes between trains.

**Clipstone-Mansfield:** As mentioned earlier, the Mansfield Railway from Clipstone to Kirkby South Junction formed an integral part of the GC trunk freight route between the south and Humberside and its freight traffic included those long-distance Annesley and Woodford freights already mentioned when referring to the Clipstone-Tuxford portion of the LD&EC. When the Hull and New Clee-Banbury fish trains were combined into one at Clipstone Sidings a portion was also detached for Mansfield Central, this being train 3M07 which departed at 9.20pm. In all the line was booked to carry 21 Up and 29 Down freights per weekday 24 hours. Its bread and butter traffic was the class 8 workings between Mansfield Concentration Sidings and Annesley(eight) or Colwick(two) with corresponding return empties. Another three class 8s a day came direct to Clipstone Sidings from Woodford Halse and one from Newstead. Dedicated trip workings, arranged in "flights," ran between Clipstone sidings and Clipstone, Mansfield, Rufford, Blidworth and Bilsthorpe collieries. In 1965, through traffic ended when Clipstone-Annesley coal trains were re-routed to the modernized Toton marshalling yard via Warsop and Shirebrook.

**Mansfield-Shireoaks.** What we now call the Robin Hood Line saw 21 booked Down freight trains in summer 1963 and 29 in the Up(southbound) direction over the section between Mansfield and Elmton & Creswell. Other trips would have run between there and Worksop serving the pits and quarries at Whitwell and Steetley. Apart from one class 7 train from Woodhouse Mill on the Midland "Old Road" to Mansfield, every booked freight was a class 8 loaded or empty mineral train. Shirebrook Sidings and the yard at Kirkby-in-Ashfield(later superseded by Toton marshalling yard) were the main reception and despatch centres. Seven workings ran each day from Shirebrook to Kirkby Sidings and three the other way. Two ran from Shirebrook Sidings

Train 4D48, loaded Merry-Go-Round test run formed of shiny new air-braked HAA hopper wagons arrives at West Burton power station early in 1965. Avery weigh specialists are on hand after coming from Sheffield in their Hillman van. West Burton coal fired station was due to close in 2020. *Tom Greaves*

to Toton. Two also ran from Warsop to Sherwood Colliery Sidings, one to Pleasley Junction, and three from Sherwood Colliery to Warsop. Trips ran to all of the collieries along the route and to pits along the South Yorkshire Joint line with no less than three from Maltby Colliery to Kirkby Sidings, as well runs serving Dinnington, Firbeck and Harworth collieries. A handful of trains ran to/from Seymour Junction via the Elmton & Creswell-Staveley line, including 8N69 from Shirebrook Sidings to Carlton Colliery(Cudworth) and two from Mansfield to Woodhouse Mill. A class 8 pick-up ran each way between Kirkby and Worksop.

Before long most of this traffic would disappear - where on earth did it all go? Onto the roads, lost with the industries which generated it, or redirected to other routes to enable closure. But coal and the big new Trent Valley power stations would keep the surviving lines - or those surviving parts of them which served collieries and power stations - busy for the next three or four decades

### The merry go round revolution

The coming of the big new Trent Valley power stations, especially those at West Burton and Cottam, east of Retford, transformed the railways of Sherwood as they were adapted to meet the challenge and new opportunities presented by the demand for a continuous supply of huge volumes of coal. Merry-go-Round working, a new diesel depot at Shirebrook in place of the old Langwith Junction steam shed, wagon repair facilities and a loco stabling point at Worksop, and the Retford underpass in place of its flat crossing, all resulted from the process of gearing up to meet the power station needs.

The first of these power stations was High Marnham, on the LD&EC east of Tuxford, a 1950s-style plant coming on stream in 1962 and using traditional rail delivery methods. It was Europe's first 1000 megawatt power station and its biggest coal fired power station when opened. In 1965 it was converted to a rapid discharge rail operation for evaluation in advance of the next generation about to open. West Burton opened in 1965 and when fully commissioned was expected to be served by 112 Brush Type 4(Class 47)-hauled 1000-ton trains a week from 14 collieries in what was BR's first full MGR operation. Cottam followed in 1968.

The power stations were purpose-built for MGR operation but at the collieries the National Coal Board was faced with having to completely rebuild its traditional loading systems at considerable expense. Thus, conversion to MGR operation was a slow process and at the start, Bevercotes was the only pit in the whole country equipped with a rapid loading facility. At other collieries MGR trains still had to be broken up and shunted by NCB locomotives in the traditional manner for loading whereas at the power stations they were being discharged without even stopping, at a speed of half a mile an hour. By the late 1960s many of Sherwood's pits were being equipped with huge rapid loading bunkers for loading MGR trains on the move and their own locomotives and internal railway systems would disappear as a result. Thus, the constant movement of MGR and traditional coal trains and returning empties along the LD&EC, through Worksop, up and down through Shirebrook and Mansfield formed the solid, and seemingly eternal backdrop to Sherwood's railways.

Of course, the 1960s brought other changes and a contraction of the local network, some of them bound up with the closure of the Great Central main line which occurred on 4th September 1966 following years of being deliberately run down, and also in line with a British Railways policy of "single sourcing" collieries. Before the railways were nationalized in 1948, each of the private companies had their own connections to collieries as they competed for traffic. But when the railways were brought under the control of one body this was no longer necessary and so BR began a programme of reducing colliery connections to just one each wherever practicable. One of the first lines to go was the former Midland branch from Shirebrook to Welbeck Colliery. Another to go was the former GN connection from the Leen Valley Extension to Shirebrook Colliery. The former Midland connection to Blidworth Colliery was also abandoned along with the Southwell line east of Rufford Colliery Junction. The Mid-Notts. Joint line was another casualty although short sections remained for shunting purposes at Bilsthorpe and Ollerton. In the longer term Clipstone, Mansfield, Rufford, Blidworth and Bilsthorpe collieries would all come to be served solely from Clipstone.

The LD&EC west of Langwith Junction was closed between Langwith Colliery and Spink Hill in 1966, the Spink Hill - Beighton Junction section being retained to serve Westthorpe Colliery. The former GN Leen Valley Extension south from Langwith Junction hung on a little longer for local freight but it too had succumbed by the end of 1968 and Langwith Junction ceased to be a junction. The LD&EC from the Warsop direction was then connected to the Mansfield-Worksop line on the Down side by a new, rather curvy, 500-yard chord descending from the former Langwith Junction to Langwith New Junction. It enabled coal trains to run direct between collieries on the LD&EC and West Burton and Cottam power stations and, interestingly, the new BR Route Code system introduced in 1972 showed Shireoaks to Lincoln Pyewipe Junction via Warsop as one route with Langwith New Junction to Mansfield and beyond as a separate route. By the start of the 1980s, the curve had been replaced by a new line on the Up side from a new Shirebrook East Junction, hewn through a new rock cutting to Warsop Junction, thus removing the bridge carrying the LD&EC over the Mansfield-Worksop line and Langwith Junction from the network altogether. Parts of the former steam motive power depot have remained in use as the wagon works of W. H. Davies, connected to the Mansfield line by a new chord rising steeply from Shirebrook Junction.

The £1 million(a hell of a lot then) Retford underpass was built so that the coal trains continuously feeding Cottam and West Burton power stations could do so without crossing the busy East Coast main line which would have been a wholly unacceptable situation leading to congestion and delays. In any case, a flat crossing on a high speed main line is hardly ideal even though another remains to this day just up the line at Newark. In this 8th October 1965 view, York 9F 2-10-0 No. 92205 rushes a northbound ECML freight over the newly completed underpass. A DMU can be seen at the new low level platform. *JBH/Colour-Rail*

The LD&EC ceased to be a through route in 1980 when it was cut back from Lincoln Pyewipe GC Junction to High Marnham following extensive damage caused by a derailment at Skellingthorpe. Other lines to go in the 1960s were the Waleswood Curve and the Pleasley Junction-Pleasley Colliery branch, the collieries around Teversal and Butcherwood from then on being served only from Tibshelf Sidings on the Erewash Valley line.

The decline of deep coal mining to the point of extinction in Britain, especially during the "Coal Crisis" of the 1990s when cheap foreign imports virtually finished off those pits which had survived the government's closure programme and the 1984/85 strike, brought a big reduction in traffic on Sherwood's surviving railways. It was during these two decades when most of the pits along these lines closed, depriving the railway of its lifeblood. Several pits linked to the LD&EC survived into the 2000s but in 2003 High Marnham power station closed and in 2015 the last of the pits, Thoresby, also closed, by which time it was one of only two deep coal mines left in the entire country. There was now no revenue-earning traffic on the LD&EC but it was far from finished. In 2009 Network Rail converted the Thoresby-High Marnham section and the Bevercotes branch into an innovative test track. Following the closure of Thoresby Colliery the remainder from Shirebrook also became part of the test track and so its future appears secure. It continues to be a focus for campaigners who want the Robin Hood Line passenger service extended to Edwinstowe and Ollerton. Shirebrook diesel depot had closed in 1997 and operations became centred on Worksop where coal trains still ran to West Burton and Cottam, but mainly with imported coal coming from Immingham and northern ports via the South Yorkshire Joint line and Brancliffe East Junction.

At the time of writing, the diesel units operating the passenger services to Sheffield, Lincoln and Nottingham have Sherwood's remaining railways almost to themselves. The sidings are all still there at Worksop, used for stabling and storing new and withdrawn passenger stock, while rows of stored wagons make a depressing sight. Cottam power station closed in September 2019 and while West Burton was still burning coal at times of peak demand at the start of 2020, coal trains were few and far between.

**The sharp gradient between Shireoaks East and Worksop West signal boxes must have posed a challenge for heavy coal trains starting out from Worksop Up Concentration Sidings, seen in the right distance, especially in steam days. Here, Doncaster-built Type 5 No. 58021 threads the maze of semaphore signals as it surmounts the gradient with power station coal for either Cottam or West Burton on Tuesday 8th July 1997.** *From a colour slide by Stephen Chapman*

RANSKILL .UP FREIGHT TRAINS REQUIRING TO STOP AT RETFORD. Drivers of Up freight trains requiring to stop specially at Retford to detach or for "loco" purposes must whistle 1 crow 2 long on passing Ranskill, and the signalman there must so advise Babworth and Retford North boxes. *BR Eastern Region Sectional Appendix January 1969*
RETFORD. When practicable Up Mineral trains must run through Retford without stopping, and drivers of such trains must in that case stop at Newark for water and examination. *BR Eastern Region Sectional Appendix January 1969*

# RETFORD G.N.

Five and a half miles north of Retford on the East Coast main line is Ranskill where there was once a British Railways regional wagon works connected to the Up side of the main line by a triangle of lines.
ABOVE: Making a true Great Northern scene, J6 0-6-0 No. 64245 shunts the wagon works yard. *Neville Stead/Transport Library*

RIGHT: The wagon works used two Sentinel locomotives listed in the Eastern Region departmental series for internal shunting. One was Class Y3 4-wheeled loco. *Departmental No.3* seen here on 26th March 1959. There isn't much that is Great Northern or even Eastern Region about this engine though. Painted over, but still fixed on the cab front are its traffic number plate displaying 68181 and its shedplate displaying the code 54B - Tyne Dock! *Neville Stead/Transport Library*

RANSKILL FACTORY SIDINGS. The two single lines between Ranskill and the Ranskill Factory Sidings are worked as sidings and movements are controlled by engine stop boards.
No train must be shunted from the Factory Sidings past the stop boards applicable to the Doncaster line and Retford Goods line unless the authority of the Shunter has been obtained. Before giving such authority the Shunter must obtain permission by telephone from the Signalman at Ranskill Station box. When the shunting movement is complete and the Single line is again clear the Shunter must advise the Signalman accordingly. The Shunter must obtain permission from the Signalman at Ranskill Station box before giving authority for a train to make a "right away" movement towards the Main line. *BR Eastern Region Sectional Appendix January 1969*

ABOVE: A 1950s class 4 fully fitted express freight headed by B1 4-6-0 No. 61266 has been turned onto the Up Goods line at Babworth on the northern approach to Retford in order to clear the main line for the southbound Flying Scotsman. On the right is Babworth goods depot which was listed in the 1956 Railway Clearing House Handbook of Stations as having a 10-ton permanent crane and able to handle general goods, livestock, furniture vans, carriages, motor cars, portable engines and machines on wheels. It closed in October 1966.

BELOW: A1 Pacific No. 60120 *Kittiwake* heads the Queen of Scots Pullman from King's Cross to Glasgow via Leeds and Harrogate past Retford's Babworth goods depot in the early 1950s. In 1924 the depot was renamed Retford Goods. *Both Alan Ashley*

**ABOVE:** One of two curves opened in 1859 so that MS&L trains could use the Great Northern station at Retford was the west-facing line to Whisker Hill Junction. With the GN station in the background and Retford North signalbox on the left, begrimed J6 0-6-0 No. 64245 heads a pick-up goods round the curve towards Whisker Hill. Nowadays, the curve is used by only a handful of Sheffield-Retford trains but between 1958 and 1968 saw four Pullman trains each day. *From a Colour-Rail colour slide.*

Below: Haring past Retford North at high speed at 4.53pm on 20th April 1960 is A3 Pacific No. 60039 *Sandwich* with the up White Rose from Leeds to King's Cross. *Robert Anderson*

**ABOVE:** Coming off the curve from Whisker Hill into Retford station is B1 4-6-0 No. 61223 with the 2.26pm Sheffield-Cleethorpes stopping service at 3.14pm on Wednesday 20th April 1960. *Robert Anderson*

**BELOW:** An Ian Allan Locospotters' Club special returning from Doncaster to Kings Cross brings unusual motive power to the ECML in the form of two locomotives preserved in active service at the time by British Railways. Great Western 4-4-0 *City of Truro* leads Midland Compound No. 1000 past Retford North at 5.50pm on 20th April 1960. Later in the journey *City of Truro* developed a hot axle box and had to be detached at Fletton Junction, just south of Peterborough. This left No.1000 and her Kentish Town crew facing the prospect of taking the 410-ton load the rest of the way to Kings Cross alone, a challenge which they met most creditably, achieving 77mph on the way. *Robert Anderson*

ABOVE: A scene from the final days of the LNER at the north end of Retford station with a V2 2-6-2 heading a southbound express while nearly brand new B1 4-6-0 No. 1211 is working the pick-up goods. *Tom Greaves*

BELOW: Memories of warm summer days at the station and trying to guess what will be the next "Streak" to appear. Bringing a moment of excitement - not that they were in short supply in steam days - A4 Pacific No. 60006 *Sir Ralph Wedgewood* was the next "Streak" through here, passing through with a non-stop express to London around 1960. *Neville Stead/Transport Library*

**ABOVE: A general view of Retford station looking north in around 1947 with another non-stop express to London, this one headed by the now preserved A4 No. 19** *Bittern. Tom Greaves*

**The next four pictures show Great Central line trains with classic GC J.G. Robinson-designed engines calling at Retford in LNER days. BELOW: A stopping service from Sheffield Victoria to either Lincoln or Cleethorpes pulls in behind D11 "Large Director" 4-4-0 No. 2666** *Zeebrugge*, **an Immingham-based loco at the time. Upon departure the train will take the curve round to Thrumpton where it will rejoin the former Great Central line.** *Tom Greaves*

*On 8th January 1955 a Sheffield Wednesday v. Hastings United FA Cup tie saw two special trains worked to Retford by A4 Pacifics Nos. 60014 Silver Link and 60017 Silver Fox. On 30th January 1960 cup tie thirteen specials ran from Peterborough to Sheffield via Retford hauled by A2 and A3 Pacifics and V2 2-6-2s. All were booked non-stop to Retford where each picked up a pilotman for the remainder of the journey. They called at Worksop for water.*

**ABOVE:** A D9 4-4-0, LNER No. 6017, calls at Retford with a Lincolnshire-bound express during the 1930s.

**BELOW:** Again, in the 1930s, Class B5 4-6-0 No. 6069 calls at the head of a Sheffield to Lincoln or Cleethorpes stopping service.
*Both Neville Stead collection/Transport Library*

**ABOVE: Class B7 4-6-0 No. 1363 awaits departure from Retford with an express from Sheffield to LIncolnshire or beyond on 8th June 1947. As with the trains in the previous three illustrations, it will take the curve round to Thrumpton on the GC line.**
*Neville Stead collection/Transport Library*

**BELOW: In the bleakest of bleak winters, A1 Pacific No. 60154 *Bon Accord* hurries the Down White Rose through Retford at 11.50am on 2nd February 1963 - just days after this service had supposedly been handed over to diesel haulage.** *Robert Anderson*

ABOVE: A3 Pacific No. 60053 *Sansovino* brings Down express No. 366 over the flat crossing and past Retford South signal box in the early 1950s. The Thrumpton spur taken by GC line trains curves away to the left. *Tom Greaves*

BELOW: Memories are made of these. Two young spotters hang on to the bridge parapet so far undisturbed by the signalman in Retford South box as LNER A3 No. 56 *Centenary* thunders a Leeds express over the flat crossing sometime around 1947. The enamel Virol advertisement stating "delicate children need it" completes the scene. What on earth was Virol? If the makers were to be believed it was certainly good stuff! *Tom Greaves*

## LOCOMOTIVES ALLOCATED TO RETFORD AT BOTH SHEDS

**SUMMER 1950: B1 4-6-0:** 61208/11/2/3/31; **O3 2-8-0:** 63475/82; **O4 2-8-0:** 63608/37/54/88/736/63/82/5/877/905/ 7/8/14; **J3 0-6-0:** 64125/33/41/8/50; **J6 0-6-0:** 64241; **J11 0-6-0:** 64280/2/7/95/306/35/40/1/7/8/80/5/93/402/13/6/21/2/3/51; **J39 0-6-0:** 64759/830/98/906/8/56/61/70/87; **J52 0-6-0ST:** 68766; **N5 0-6-2T:** 69273/7/82/94/313/21/54. **Total: 63**

**JULY 1962: 350hp 0-6-0:** D3612-20; **Ivatt 4MT 2-6-0:** 43157; **B1 4-6-0:** 61120/6/1208/11/12/13/25/31; **K1 2-6-0:** 62015/9/37/9/40/51/4/67/70; **O4 2-8-0:** 63586/602/32/7/47/55/65/72/88/702/4/ 18/26/7/36/64/71/85/818/24/908/14; **O2 2-8-0:** 63924/5/6/7/36/7/9/45/6/61/4/5/6/9/71/2/3/5/6/79/80/3/6/7; **J11 0-6-0:** 64324/32/54. **Total: 76**

Retford had two motive power depots, the former Great Central one at Thrumpton and the former Great Northern shed alongside Retford station. They were both treated as one depot and in BR days were coded 36E under the overlordship of Doncaster. Both depots supplied mainly goods engines but also had an allocation of shunting engines and some mixed traffic types. The sheds were rebuilt by British Railways in the 1950s but closed altogether in June 1965. ABOVE: On 16th August 1959 B1 4-6-0 No. 61211 boils on the 4-road former GN shed alongside Retford station.
*Neville Stead/Transport Library*

LEFT: The world's fastest steam locomotive on Retford shed. Just why A4 Pacific No. 60022 *Mallard* came on shed on 14th May 1956 rather than passing through as it normally did is not recorded. Perhaps it arrived on a special working for Sheffield to be relieved by a local engine as sometimes occurred.
*Stephen Chapman archive*

**ABOVE: Simmering in the shed yard with the coal stage behind it and the station beyond on 30th April 1962 is Class O2/4 2-8-0 No. 63924. Retford shed was noted for its sizeable allocation of these Gresley-designed GN goods engines - this one actually a version rebuilt by Thompson from 1943.** *Neville Stead collection/Transport Library*

**BELOW: In 1934 Retford GN shed was equipped with a water softening plant which could process 7500 gallons a minute supplied from the shed's original giant water tank. An out of use K1 2-6-0 sits forlornly on a siding sandwiched between the turntable and the water tank(right) and water softener(left.)** *Stephen Chapman archive*

**ABOVE:** Looking south along the East Coast main line from Retford South signal box in the 1950s a WD 2-8-0 is seen approaching the flat crossing with a Down Through Freight. *Tom Greaves*

**BELOW:** The Great Northern still rules in this 1930s scene. Just south of Retford, one of H. A. Ivatt's Class C1 Atlantics, LNER No. 3289, has just emerged from the 57-yard Askham Tunnel and is passing a classic GN somersault signal as it heads an Up express.
*Neville Stead collection/Transport Library*

**ABOVE:** Near Markham, the world's most famous engine, A3 Pacific No. 60103 *Flying Scotsman*, still with its single chimney, heads a 1950s express. *Stephen Chapman archive*

**BELOW:** Five and a half miles south of Retford came Tuxford North station, seen here as A3 No. 60066 *Merry Hampton* sweeps through with a London express on 24th May 1959. Tuxford North goods depot, was run jointly by the LNER and LMS(formerly LNWR which reached it via Bottesford North Junction and Newark. It was listed in 1938 as having a 5-ton permanent crane and able to handle all classes of goods, except the LMS could not handle horse boxes, cattle vans, motors cars or carriage trucks by passenger train. The station closed to passengers from 4th July 1955 and to goods on 15th June 1964. *Neville Stead collection/Transport Library*

RIGHT: It is hard to grasp that in 1975 when this view is dated, that there were still gated level crossings and signal boxes on the 100mph East Coast main line like this one at Tuxford where the box has taken on the characteristics of a dilapidated greenhouse. But with 125mph trains less than three years away, they would have to go and the High Speed Running programme and resignalling saw the crossing replaced by a bridge and the box eliminated. *Stephen Chapman archive*

LEFT: Dukeries Junction, looking south. This is where the LD&EC intersects with the ECML, by means of the overbridge in the distance. The lines on the right go up to Tuxford West Junction, allowing trains to travel between the the LD&EC and the ECML while exchange sidings are sited between the two routes. Passing over the junction is A2/2 Pacific No. 60502 *Earl Marischal* with the Down Queen of Scots at 2.10pm on 20th August 1960. *David Holmes*
Today all is gone except for the two electrified running lines and a pair of emergency crossovers, while the LD&EC survives as a test track.

RIGHT: The two-level station at Dukeries Junction. At ground level are the former GN platforms with the island platform on the bridge serving the LD&EC. There were no goods facilities and the whole lot was closed to passengers with effect from 6th March 1950, *Stephen Chapman archive*

# RETFORD - WOODHOUSE

Class 04/8 2-8-0 No. 63738 heads past Thrumpton signal box and the malthouses in the direction of Gainsborough with a class 7 coal train, possibly bound for Immingham, on 10th July 1963. *K.C.H. Fairey/Colour-Rail*

## RETFORD THRUMPTON TO WOODHOUSE EAST JUNCTION
*BRITISH RAILWAYS EASTERN REGION SECTIONAL APPENDIX 18th JANUARY 1969*

**SIGNALLING:** Track Circuit Block Gainsborough Trent Jn. - Manton Wood.
Absolute Block Manton Wood-Woodhouse East Jn. Permissive Block on Goods lines.

**MAXIMUM SPEED: On Main Lines:** 60mph

**LOOPS AND REFUGE SIDINGS:** Up and Down Goods Loops at Retford Thrumpton; Down Refuge Siding with standage for 60 wagons, engine and brake van at Manton Wood; Down Refuge Siding with standage for 35 wagons, engine and brake van at Worksop East; Up and Down Goods lines Worksop West-Shireoaks East; Additional Up Goods line Worksop West Sidings-Shireoaks East; Up Refuge Siding with standage for 50 wagons, engine and brake van at Shireoaks Station; Down Refuge Siding with standage for 48 wagons, engine and brake at Kiveton Park Colliery; Up Refuge Siding with standage for 36 wagons, engine and brake van at Brookhouse Colliery.

**SIGNAL BOXES**(with distance from previous box): Thrumpton Crossing(1 mile 1370 yds from West Burton;) Manton Wood(5miles 1166yds;) Worksop East(1 mile 1688yds;) Worksop West(502yds;) Shireoaks East Junction (545yds;) Shireoaks Station(1 mile 139yds;) Brancliffe East Junction 1741yds;) Kiveton Park Station(2 miles 140yds;) Kiveton Park Colliery(1355yds;) Waleswood Junction(2 miles 181yds;) Brookhouse Colliery(1043yds;) Woodhouse East Junction(1 mile 927yds.)

**Retford Thrumpton** goods depot was listed in the 1956 Railway Clearing House Handbook of Stations as having a 5-ton capacity permanent crane and equipped to handle general goods, furniture vans, carriages, motor cars, portable engines, machines on wheels and livestock. Originally Retford, it was renamed Thrumpton in March 1924 and closed with effect from 7th December 1970 after having been reduced to a Public Delivery Siding.
Private sidings served The Bee Hive Works of W. J. Jenkings & Co. gas engineers and iron founders also manufacturing coal preparation and coking works plant; J. Pidcock & Co. Ltd. maltsters; E. Sutcliffe Ltd. maltsters who also had maltings at Worksop and Kiveton Bridge; and J. W. Holmes Ltd. There were also Ordsall and Rushey Public Delivery Sidings.
Private sidings listed in 1938 were E. Sutcliffe Ltd.; and Worksop & Retford Brewery Co.

**ABOVE:** Retford's twin motive power depots were each of modest size but together they made a fairly large depot. This is the three-road Great Central shed at Thrumpton as rebuilt with a "northlight" roof, and where Gresley GN design of 1911 J6 0-6-0 No. 64236 is seen standing at the west end on 22nd July 1960. *K.C.H. Fairey/Colour-Rail*

**BELOW:** In common with most GC depots, Thrumpton had a set of sheerlegs which were at the east end of the yard. This scene shows O4/8 2-8-0 No. 63914 in steam under the sheerlegs on 24th August 1963 while O2/3 No. 63975, also in steam, is parked alongside.
*From a Colour-Rail colour slide*

**ABOVE:** The classic view of Retford GC shed yard from London Road on 16th August 1959. The stabling sidings are well filled with goods engines, some in steam, some dead, mainly of classes O2 and O4 while O1 No. 63795 from Staveley is in the left foreground and a WD 2-8-0 simmers at the far end of the line. To the right of the nearest two rows of engines can be seen Retford's allocated 15-ton steam crane, No. 108 which had a route availability of 7, reduced to 6 in an emergency. The malthouses dominate the skyline and on the far right is the goods yard, stocked with coal wagons. *Neville Stead/Transport Library.*

**BELOW:** It was never all goods engines at Retford GC shed as this picture can testify. On 13th April 1947 during the final months of the LNER a brace of ex-GC Class C4 Atlantics, superheated C4/4 No. 2923 nearest, were to be found stabled in front of the coal stage. *Stephen Chapman archive*

LEFT: At the east end of the yard is J11 0-6-0 No. 64421 along with a J6 0-6-0. *Stephen Chapman archive*

Below: One of Retford's ex-Great Northern J3 0-6-0s, No. 64125, rests in the loco yard on 31st May 1953. These engines were Gresley 1912 rebuilds of Ivatt's 1896 J4s, which in turn were a development of earlier Stirling 0-6-0s By a quirk of fate, when the LNER renumbered its fleet in 1946, the then 4125 kept the same number. *Neville Stead collection/Transport Library*

BELOW: Meat and drink for the J11s was goods and mineral trip working on the former Great Central lines. This signalman's view at Retford South shows No. 64402 heading away from Thrumpton and onto the flat crossing over the ECML with a westbound trip in the 1950s.
On the left is the curve from the GN station complete with its timber platform extension for use by GC line trains. *Tom Greaves*

**ABOVE:** One can almost hear the thunder and feel the vibration as B17/1 4-6-0 No. 61621 *Hatfield House* passes Retford South box with the non-stop Liverpool-Harwich boat train in the 1950s. The vantage point provides a rare view of the driver at his post. *Tom Greaves*

**BELOW:** Between the flat crossing and Whisker Hill Junction came West Sidings where O4/8 2-8-0 No. 63785 is busy shunting on the Down side. The main running lines are to the left of the engine. *Neville Stead collection/Transport Library*

ABOVE: At Whisker Hill Junction, Brush Type 4 prototype No. D0280 *Falcon* brings the King's Cross to Sheffield Pullman round the curve from Retford station and on to the GC line in 1962. Retford West Sidings are just right of the signal box. The open land behind *Falcon* used to be a rail-connected sand pit. *Peter Cookson* The Sheffield Pullmans were advertised to call at Retford en-route to London at 7.18am(The Master Cutler) and at 3.53pm(not Saturdays,) and from London at 5.58pm(not Saturdays) and 9.31pm(The Master Cutler) - two return trips Monday to Friday, one on Saturday.

BELOW: A long empty wagon train is hauled westbound near Checker House by O4/8 2-8-0 No. 63801 - recently rebuilt from 04/3 - in the evening of 22nd May 1957. *Mike Mitchell/Transport Treasury*. There was a station here with a goods yard consisting of a loop with a cattle dock and two sidings with a small goods shed and weighbridge but no crane. It was listed in the 1938 Handbook of Stations as able to handle general goods, livestock, horse boxes and prize cattle vans. Between Checker House and Retford was a siding serving a brick works which had closed by 1920 and Rushey public siding. Checker House station closed to passengers in September 1931. The goods yard closed on 1st October 1956 but was reopened on 31st October 1960, and finally closed in December 1963.

ABOVE: At Manton Wood Junction were connections into Manton Wood Colliery. With no rapid loading bunker, ex-BR Drewry Class 04 0-6-0 shunter No. D2229 pushes MGR hoppers under the conventional loading screens on 21st May 1987. In BR service, this engine was at 31B March. Manton Wood Colliery closed in 1994. *Adrian Booth*

BELOW: Between Manton Wood and Worksop the line crosses Retford Road and the Chesterfield Canal on a long, low viaduct. On 19th February 1988, BR Type 5 No. 58033 passes over the canal with an empty MGR train returning from one of the power stations. *From a colour slide by Adrian Booth*

**ABOVE:** Worksop East signal box is on the left as Immingham-based K3 2-6-0 No. 61866 restarts a summer Saturday extra to the coast from Worksop station on 14th June 1959. Interesting to note that there were once two footbridges, one on the station and one for the level crossing. Today only the station has a bridge. *Neville Stead/Transport Library*

**LEFT:** By way of a change from coal trains, a regular sand train ran from East Anglia to glass works at Kirk Sandall (Doncaster) and Monk Bretton(Barnsley) via Worksop and the South Yorkshire Joint line. On the way, it detached wagons at Worksop glass works situated next to appropriately-named Sandhole Sidings. The train still ran at the time of writing but not via Worksop. At 13.06 on 8th July 1997 58046 passes Worksop East signal box with the Middleton Towers-Kirk Sandall train. The 20-lever Worksop East box is an MS&L design dating from c1880 and re-framed in 1975. *From a colour slide by Stephen Chapman*

A Derby Works Class 108 DMU calls at Worksop with a Sheffield-Lincoln service on 3rd May 1991.
*From a colour slide by Stephen Chapman*

**WORKSOP LOCO-HAULED PASSENGER TRAINS Saturdays August 1959**

| am | Down direction | am | Up direction |
|---|---|---|---|
| 7.52 | 7.35 Retford-Sheffield class B | 3.40 | 1.50 Manchester London Rd.-Cleethorpes |
| 11.03 | 9.14 Cleethorpes-Manchester London Rd. | Pass | 5.45 Wadsley Bridge-Woodhall Junction |
| 11.38 | 9.43 Cleethorpes-Manchester London Rd. | 6.55 | 6.14 Sheffield Victoria-Boston class B |
| 12.38 | 9.25 Cambridge-Manchester Central | Pass | 7.20 Sheffield Victoria-Kings Cross Pullman *The Master Cutler* |
| Pass | 8.0 Harwich Parkeston Quay-Liverpool Central | | |
| **pm** | | 7.55 | 7.24 Sheffield Victoria-Cleethorpes |
| 1.46 | 11.33am Skegness-Sheffield Victoria | 8.25 | 7.50 Sheffield Victoria-Yarmouth Vauxhall |
| 2.5 | 11.47am Skegness-Manchester Central | Pass | 7.10 Tibshelf Town-Skegness |
| Pass | 9.17am Yarmouth Vauxhall-Sheffield Victoria | 9.47 | 9.15 Sheffield Victoria-Skegness |
| 3.0 | 12.3 Skegness-Sheffield Victoria | 10.40 | 8.40 Manchester Central-Sutton on Sea |
| 3.48 | 2.0 Cleethorpes-Sheffield Victoria | 10.48 | 9.10 Manchester London Rd.-Skegness |
| Pass | 1.47 Skegness-Tibshelf Town | 11.10 | 9.30 Manchester London Rd.-Cleethorpes |
| 4.12 | 11.16am Yarmouth Vauxhall-Manchester Central | 11.23 | 9.25 Manchester Central-Norwich & Yarmouth |
| 4.25 | 4.10 Retford-Sheffield Victoria class B | 11.42 | 10.10 Manchester London Rd.-Cleethorpes |
| 4.37 | 11.43am Yarmouth Vauxhall/Norwich-Sheffield Vic. | **pm** | |
| 5.5 | 2.52 Skegness-Sheffield Victoria | 3.32 | 1.45 Manchester Central-Cambridge |
| 5.41 | 3.10 Mablethorpe & Sutton on Sea-Manchester Cen. | 3.58 | 1.15 Liverpool Central-Harwich Town |
| Pass | 3.10 Kings Cross-Sheffield Pullman | 4.19 | 3.40 Sheffield Victoria-Lincoln Central class B |
| 6.20 | 4.20 Woodhall Junction-Wadsley Bridge | 5.33 | 3.15 Manchester Central-Cleethorpes class B |
| 7.33 | 6.38 Lincoln Central-Sheffield Victoria | 6.59 | 5.0 Manchester London Rd.-Cleethorpes class B |
| 7.54 | 5.18 Boston-Sheffield Victoria class B | 9.30 | 8.52 Sheffield Victoria-Gainsborough Central class B |
| 8.21 | 6.30 Cleethorpes-Sheffield Victoria | | |
| 9.53 | 9.37 Retford-Manchester London Rd. | | |

*Nottingham-Worksop trains were also loco-hauled. Besides the above were the normal Sheffield-Cleethorpes and Lincoln local services which were now operated by DMUs. Manchester London Road was renamed Piccadilly the following year.*

**ABOVE:** 9F 2-10-0 No. 92202 passes the goods warehouse while approaching Worksop station on 10th September 1963 with an eastbound class 8 Through Freight. *From a Colour-Rail colour slide by JBH.* Worksop goods depot was listed in 1956 as having a 10-ton capacity permanent crane and able to handle all classes of freight. The warehouse was demolished in the 1980s but the goods yard remained in business at least until closure of the Speedlink wagonload freight network in the early 1990s.

**BELOW:** The single-car Class 153 on a Doncaster-Lincoln service(via Sheffield!) allows a clear view of the splendid display of semaphore signals on the approach from the west - possibly the best remaining in the entire country by then - that a full length train would obscure. Just beyond 153315 is Worksop West signal box, an original MS&L structure of 1874 with a 28-lever frame which was renewed c1928. Beyond that, also on the right, are Worksop Up Concentration Sidings and on the left are the Down sidings. In the distance is Shireoaks East box. In the left foreground are the weed-covered goods yard sidings. The date is 23rd April 1997 and within five years the semaphores would be just a memory. *From a colour slide by Stephen Chapman*

**RIGHT:** As part of the move towards Merry-Go-Round coal working, a new wagon maintenance depot was established at Sandhole Sidings which hastened the closure of other regional shops at Ranskill and Tuxford. On 26th February 1988, 350hp 0-6-0 No. 08824 is seen positioning wagons. *From a colour slide by Adrian Booth*

With MGR operations becoming increasingly centred on Worksop a new train crew depot was opened here in 1991 with crews transferring from Shirebrook and Barrow Hill.

**BELOW:** A Class 47 diesel has taken charge of a train of MGR hoppers in the Down yard in August 1980 as a pair of class 31s on the Up side head a train of air-braked HBA hopper wagons used for coke and non-power station coal. *Malcolm Roughley/Stephen Chapman archive.* By 1965, the 9F 2-10-0s and various 2-8-0s had given way to Class 20, 31 and 37 diesels with specially adapted Class 47s on the power station workings. By the late 1970s new class 56s were taking over the MGR jobs, followed by the 1980s Class 58s and finally the Class 66s brought in by the private operators.

**The 1956 Handbook of Stations listed Worksop** as having no less than 15 private sidings. A number were connected with glass and tile making reflecting the area's history of sand and clay quarrying. The sidings were for: Batchelors Peas Ltd; Co-op Wholesale Society Ltd. glassworks; Jas. Turner & Sons Ltd.; General Refractories Ltd; S. Aldred & Co. chemical works, via General Refractories siding; Godley & Goulding Ltd.; National Coal Board Manton Colliery; Newtons(Worksop) Ltd; G. G. Middleton Ltd., via Newtons siding; Oates Ltd; C. E. Seed Ltd.; E. Sutcliffe & Co. Ltd. maltsters Clinton Siding and Eastgate Siding; George Turton, Platts & Co. Ltd.; Worksop Corporation.

GENERAL REFRACTORIES LTD. - SIDINGS. When wagons are being propelled into this siding the brakes on the leading wagon must be pinned down at the gate. When wagons are being drawn out of the siding the speed must not exceed 4mph and the Shunter must walk beside the last wagon ready to apply the brakes if necessary. The firm's permission must be obtained before entering the siding. *BR Eastern Region Section Appendix 18th January 1969.*

**ABOVE:** It has to be admitted there are an awful lot of diesel locomotives in this section but they are now as much a part of the past as steam. **In August 1980 a Class 47 positions MGR wagons in the Down yard.** *Malcolm Roughly/Stephen Chapman archive*

**BELOW: Class 20s rule in the Up Concentration Sidings in August 1980 where the traffic at this time appears to be mostly conventional in nature, including traditional 16-ton mineral wagons. Before long there would be a drive by BR to eliminate these short wheelbase vehicles.** *Malcolm Roughly/Stephen Chapman archive*

**Reception roads west end of Worksop Up Sidings,** Working through shunting neck. The signalman at Shireoaks East Junction box must not allow trains consisting of more than 45 wagons from No.1 Loop line, or more than 50 wagons from No.2 Loop line to be set back towards the Foreman Shunter or other person in charge of the Up sidings unless advised that one of the Reception lines is sufficiently clear to admit of the engine propelling the train passing beyond Shireoaks East Junction box before it is necessary for it to be brought to a stand. When trains are being set back the Foreman Shunter or other person in charge of the Up sidings must see that the requisite hand signals are given to the Drivers, who must in all cases keep a good look out for such signals. When wagons are being run off the Foreman Shunter...is responsible for seeing the points leading up to the slip line are set for that line..*Eastern Region Sectional Appendix 1969*

**Worksop West.** Engines not booked to take water at the Down side column were prohibited from doing so and drivers were instructed to take enough water before reaching Worksop to see them beyond that point. If they needed water there in an emergency they had to give one long and three short whistles when passing Rushey Siding signal box, the signalman there being instructed to inform Worksop East and West boxes.

RIGHT: The GC 35-lever Shireoaks East Junction signal box dating from 1914, seen on 23rd April 1997.
*Stephen Chapman*

BELOW: Former BR 204hp shunters were to be found at a number of collieries in this area. This is Class 04 No. D2332 at Shireoaks Colliery on 2nd September 1982.
*From a colour slide by Adrian Booth*

BOTTOM: Looking east from the footbridge at Shireoaks station during the late 1960s while what appears to be an enthusiats' special hauled by a Brush Type 2 calls there. On the left is the small goods yard which comprised two sidings, one with a cattle dock, until closing in December 1963 and by this time used for stabling purposes. The lines going off to the right just beyond the level crossing lead to the Roundabout Reception sidings referred to on page 47. One of the earliest pits in the area being opened in 1859, Shireoaks closed in 1990.
*Stephen Chapman archive*

*On Saturday 17th June 1972* three private 9-coach loco-hauled excursions were run from Woodhouse to Cleethorpes and back on behalf of the Woodhouse Central Club. Outward they were 1G11 07.04 ex-Woodhouse; 1G12 07.20 ex-Woodhouse and 1G13 07.34 ex-Woodhouse, booked to pass Worksop at 07.21, 07.38 and 07.48 respectively. The return workings were due past Worksop at 18.15, 18.36 and 19.18.

ABOVE: B1 4-6-0 No. 61166 from Mexborough shed shunts the stock of a Railway Correspondence and Travel Society railtour at Shireoaks station on 11th May 1952.
*Neville Stead collection/Transport Library*

ABOVE AND RIGHT: Shireoaks station and signal box looking towards Worksop on 24th June 1997. Although unstaffed, Shireoaks retained its buildings which are of special architectural interest. Notice the unusual portico in the Down side buildings on the right. The signal box is another MS&L box from 1874 but re-equipped with a switch panel in 1980. *Stephen Chapman*

ABOVE: At Shireoaks on 7th June 1953 with D11 4-4-0 No. 62667 *Somme* of 40F Boston shed on the RCTS South Yorkshire Railtour No.2. *Neville Stead collection/Transport Library*

SHIREOAKS COLLIERY. There are three sets of points concerned in a setting back movement from the shunt neck to the Roundabout Reception Siding and staff must ensure that these points are in the correct position....A Stop Board is positioned at the entrance to the Roundabout Reception Sidings worded: "British Railways Engines must not pass this point." A warning treadle is situated near the gantry over the Roundabout Reception Sidings and Colliery run-round road. Guards when disposing of empty wagons must satisfy themselves that the wagons are left clear of the treadle. The Shireoaks Station signalman must inform Guards into which siding empty wagons are to be placed. Empty wagons must not be placed on the colliery loaded weigh line which is next on the left to the New Line Roundabout Reception Sidings...*BR Eastern Region Sectional Appendix 1969*

ABOVE: Brancliffe East Junction viewed from a public footpath crossing on Friday 21st November 1997 when resignalling was under way. The 25-lever signal box is a Great Central structure dating from 1905. The South Yorkshire Joint line to Dinnington, Maltby and Doncaster curves away to the right. *From a colour slide by Stephen Chapman*

ABOVE: A Toton-Hellifield railtour approaches Kiveton Park from the east headed by Sulzer Type 2s Nos. 25060 and 25047 on 16th March 1987. *From a colour slide by Stephen Chapman.*

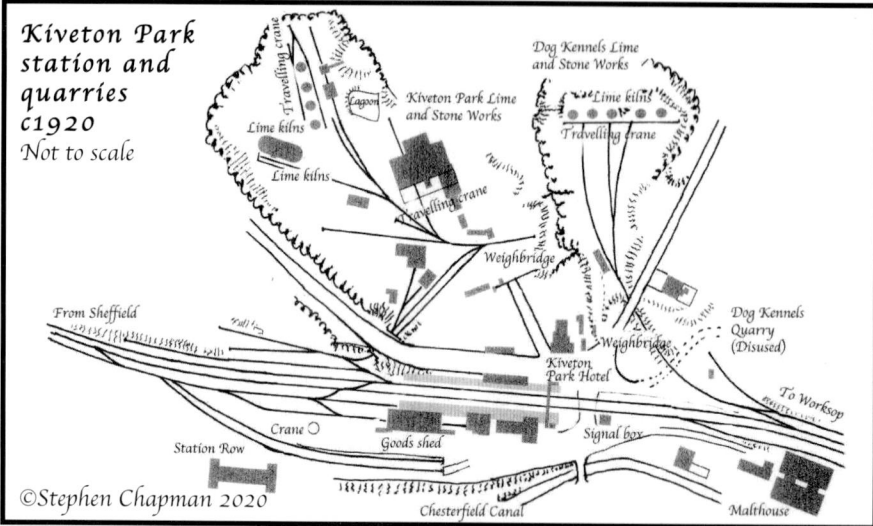

The station goods yard at **Kiveton Park** was listed in 1956 as having a 5-ton capacity permanent crane and equipped to handle general goods, livestock, and horse boxes and prize cattle vans. Goods facilities were withdrawn with effect from 14th June 1965. Kiveton Park passenger station remains open, unstaffed since 29th June 1969.

Besides the National Coal Board Kiveton Park Colliery, private sidings at Kiveton Park served Scaife & Sons' Lime Siding and E. Sutcliffe Ltd.'s malt kilns.

LEFT: On 16th March 1985 the approach to Kiveton Park Colliery was heralded by this collection of disused diesel shunters. Two are ex-BR Class 04 0-6-0s, the furthest one being D2322, and a Hudswell Clarke 0-6-0. The cab of another loco can be seen behind them. *From a colour slide by Stephen Chapman*

ABOVE: The railways of Sherwood have always been a popular venue for railtours. Here, in August 1966 Wakefield-allocated B1 No. 61131 is blasting through Kiveton Park station with a Down RCTS special. *From a Colour-Rail colour slide*

BELOW: Kiveton Park Colliery on 8th August 1980 with Brush Type 4 No. 47371 passing at the head of an eastbound loaded MGR. coal train. One of the pit's ex-BR diesel shunters waits in the colliery yard on the left. Until 1969 Kiveton Park Colliery was also served by a branch from Killamarsh Branch Junction on the former Midland "Old Road." The train has just passed Kiveton Bridge station which was nearer the colliery than Kiveton Park station. The pit closed in 1994. *From a colour slide by Adrian Booth*

ABOVE: Waleswood station with its timber platforms and buildings looking east. This station closed to passengers on 7th March 1955. There were no goods facilities but sidings once served the NCB's Waleswood Colliery and Briquetting Works which was situated behind the station on the right, the sidings just visible beyond the platform. *Jim Hatcher*

CENTRE: Waleswood Junction was followed by Brookhouse Colliery and coking plant, a large and complex site which was also served by a spur from the former Midland Railway "Old Road." Controlling the connections with the GC Sheffield-Retford line was Brookhouse Colliery signal box. Under the watch of the signal box, Brush Type 2s Nos. 31274 and 31271 head a load of coke at the colliery sidings on 3rd November 1978. *From a colour slide by Adrian Booth*

BOTTOM: Out of use in the yard at Brookhouse Colliery on 12th March 1972 was this Hawthorn Leslie 0-6-0ST, builders No. 3726. *Adrian Booth*

ABOVE: A general view of Brookhouse Colliery looking east on 3rd November 1978 with ex-BR Class 04 shunter No. D2229 and a permanent way gang the only apparent signs of rail activity. Brookhouse Colliery was established on the site of the rail loading screens and sidings for North Staveley Colliery which was up to the left and linked to the screens by an internal tramway passing over the Sheffield-Worksop line in the left distance. Brookhouse pit closed in 1985. *Adrian Booth*

BELOW: A busier scene at Brookhouse in 1976 with a Yorkshire Engine Co. "Janus" 0-6-0 diesel electric, builder's No. 2754 of 1960, on shunting duty at the plant of the United Coke & Chemical Company, a part of the British Steel Corporation. The works was situated just south west of the colliery and backed onto the North Staveley Curve which connected the Sheffield-Retford line with the Midland "Old Road." *Adrian Booth*

ABOVE: Things come to life at Brookhouse Colliery on 3rd November 1978 as D2229 gets down to work.

LEFT: These odd looking beasts are the 0-4-0 electric locomotives that worked the Brookhouse coking plant coke car used to collect fresh coke from the ovens. Seen on 28th December 1976 they were built by the Wellman, Smith, Owen Engineering Corporation Ltd. of Darlaston, Staffordshire. The one on the left is active at the ovens while the one on the right is spare.
*Both Adrian Booth*

RIGHT: On a wintry 3rd January 1977, a two-car Class 114 Derby Works DMU forming a Sheffield-Lincoln service passes the Swallownest shaft of Brookhouse Colliery on the site of Beighton Colliery, which had been combined with Brookhouse Colliery in the 1950s. In the valley beyond is the former Midland "Old Road" from Chesterfield to Rotherham and beyond that, in the mist, is Beighton permanent way yard and then Woodhouse East Junction. *Adrian Booth*

# TUXFORD-LANGWITH JN.-KILLAMARSH

ABOVE: WD 2-8-0 No. 90224 passes Tuxford West with a long train of 21-ton hopper wagons in the early 1960s. *Tom Greaves.*

Tuxford engine shed, coded 40D in the Lincoln district in BR days, and the accompanying workshops, were once the heart of the LD&EC Railway. Tuxford provided goods engines for LD&EC mineral workings but with the development and expansion of Langwith Junction shed, Tuxford's star soon began to fade. Oddly, there was no turntable and one can only assume that if an engine needed turning it had to go to the triangle at Clipstone. The shed close in 1957 and staff were transferred to Langwith Junction for which a one-coach train - the "DIDO" - ran each day taking them to and from work there. After closure, the Tuxford West pilot, which worked 6.35am to 2pm Monday to Friday was provided by Retford shed.
The view above shows the three-road building consisting of the maintenance shed on the right and the by then roofless two-road running shed with the water tank and water softener on the left. It is 12th May 1956 and a selection of former GC 2-8-0s and 0-6-0s make up the engines on shed. *K.C.H. Fairey/Colour-Rail.*

**LOCOMOTIVES ALLOCATED TO TUXFORD JUNE 1955. O1 2-8-0:** 63607/83/893; **O4 2-8-0:** 63597/622/35/43/91/722/58/912; **J11 0-6-0:** 64299/344/53/92/424. **Total: 16**

ABOVE: J11 0-6-0 No. 64424 stands outside the shed in the early 1950s. Comparison with the picture on page 53 shows that much of the roof was removed shortly before closure. *Eric Sawford/Transport Treasury*

BELOW: A Great Northern incursion at Tuxford shed. C12 4-4-2T No. 67352 appears to have been put out to grass at the back of the shed in this view on 25th September 1949. This was not the end of the road for 67352, however, as it was then allocated to New England for working the Stamford branch. In the cutting behind it is the East Coast main line and wagons can be seen in the Dukeries Junction exchange sidings. *Neville Stead collection/Transport Library*

**ABOVE: LNER Class N6 No. 5066, one of the original LD&EC 0-6-2Ts at Tuxford West sidings in 1934.** *N. Stead colln./Transport Library*

**ABOVE:** Although the shed closed in 1957, the works survived repairing wagons well into the 1960s and a 204hp 0-6-0 diesel shunter was noted there as pilot in 1963. While bearing little relation to its much bigger neighbour at Doncaster, this works was also known locally as "The Plant." The abandoned workshops are seen here in 1975.

**RIGHT:** Tuxford West signal box with the curve from Dukeries Junction coming in from the right. *Both Stephen Chapman archive*

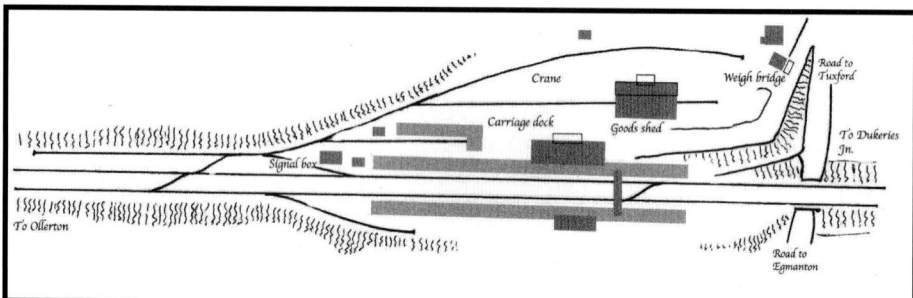

**ABOVE: WD 2-8-0 No. 90418 shunts Shellmex-BP oil tanks in Tuxford Central goods yard in September 1964.** *From a H.N.James/Colour-Rail colour slide*

**Tuxford Central** was listed in the 1938 Railway Clearing House Handbook of Stations as having a 3-ton permanent crane and able to handle all classes of goods. The station was closed to both passengers and goods from 19th September 1955 but reopened as a public siding in 1957. The oil terminal was opened at that time and a grain terminal was also established on the site.

**Tuxford Central station and signal box from a westbound train on 2nd September 1955.** *Stephen Chapman archive*

LEFT: Boughton station looking east from a westbound train on 2nd September 1955. The station served the neighbouring military depot and must have been used by many service personnel during the 1940s and 50s. The small goods yard behind the signal box was listed in 1938 as having a 3-ton crane and able to handle all types of traffic. Boughton closed to passengers from 19th September 1955 and to goods in January 1965 but the sidings were retained for a time to serve the Butterley brickworks.
*Stephen Chapman archive*

ABOVE: A rare view looking east from the bridge carrying the Mid-Notts Joint line over the LD&EC on 27th April 1957. The rather modest Boughton Sidings signal cabin is down below on the right. Behind the line of huts and trees in the middle distance is the War Department depot, the sidings connected with it being just to the right of the white building right of the line of trees. The white patch on the hillside above is the Butterley Brick Co.'s works. The sidings down below form the eastern extremity of Ollerton Colliery sidings. *Colour-Rail*

Once over the bridge, this section of the Mid-Notts was joined by a north-facing spur from Ollerton Colliery Sidings. With the line not completed the spur led nowhere and was subsequently lifted and the line over the bridge used for wagon storage until being removed by 1971.

## THE MID-NOTTS JOINT LINE

The Mid-Notts LNER/LMS joint line from Ollerton to Farnsfield was a single track 7 miles 1677 yards long. The LMS/Joint line boundary was 1¼ miles north of Farnsfield at a spot called Farnsfield Curve Jn. suggesting that a Mansfield-facing curve was intended.

Signalling was by Electric Token Block between Farnsfield and Bilsthorpe signal boxes. A blue key token was used Farnsfield-Bilsthorpe. The Bilsthorpe-New Ollerton section was worked according to One Engine in Steam regulations using a triangular red staff with Bilsthorpe the staff station. In both cases, signalmen were the persons authorized to deliver the token and staff to/and received the token and staff from the driver

The March 1937 LMS Sectional Appendix stated: "The direction of the Up line is from Ollerton Colliery Empty Wagon Sidings and from Ollerton Colliery Loaded Wagon Sidings to the main line."

A 1380-yard branch went from Bilsthorpe to Bilsthorpe Empty Wagon Sidings worked according to One Engine in Steam regulations using a round black staff. The 1937 Sectional Appendix stated: "Until further notice the staff section will end at the colliery end of the run-round loop." As with many freight only lines the precise date of closure is difficult to pin down. The Farnsfield-Bilsthorpe section was shown in the 1969 BR Sectional Appendix as worked by Electric Token Farnsfield Station-Bilsthorpe(2 miles 313yds,) and One Engine in Steam Bilsthorpe-Bilsthorpe Colliery Empty Wagon Sidings(1380yds.).

**New Ollerton.** All wagons must be taken in front of the engine from Ollerton empty wagon branch run-round loop to the empty wagon sidings. The points in the empty wagon branch leading to the screen lines must always be kept locked open for the screen lines, except when required to be unlocked to allow trains to pass between the branch line and empty wagon sidings.
*LMS Sectional Appendix March 1937*

**LEFT:** Doncaster BREL-built Type 5 No. 58038 between the colliery (right) and the smokeless fuel plant at Ollerton in 1986. Why it is on the "wrong road" is not recorded. *From a Stephen Chapman archive colour slide*

*In 1976 Ollerton Colliery* was listed as having the following NCB diesel locomotives for shunting the colliery and smokeless fuel plant: No. D1 Hudswell Clarke 0-6-0 D961 of 1956, D8 Rolls Royce 10257 of 1966, D15 Rolls Royce 10262 of 1967, D26 Rolls Royce 10193 of 1964, and Rolls Royce 10270 of 1967.

After a rapid loading bunker for MGR operation was installed in the 1980s, Rolls Royce 10270 - numbered 47453 - was retained for shunting work until 1990 at least.

Ollerton Colliery closed in 1994.

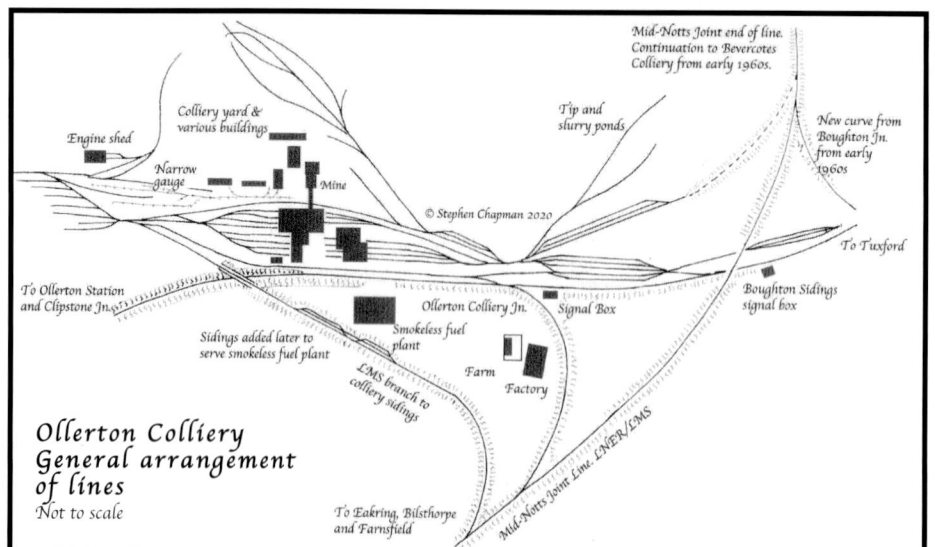

**Ollerton Colliery Down Sidings.** When it is necessary for a train to proceed to or from the sidings, the person in charge of the train must obtain the Annetts Key for working the points from the Down Main to the sidings, from the signal box and after the train has passed over the points, the points must be replaced to their normal position and the Annetts Key returned to the signal box. When propelling empty freight vehicles in the Eakring direction, care must be exercised in crossing the four occupation crossings.

Before the line between the connection to the former LMR loaded line and the double sided notice board 450 yards on the Eakring side of the National Carbonising Company's line connection is occupied by a train either from the Eakring direction, from the LMR loaded line, or from the National Carbonising Company's line, the person in charge must ascertain that this portion of line is clear before requesting the permission of the signalman to occupy it. *BR Eastern Region Sectional Appendix January 1969*

**ABOVE:** This NCB 0-6-0ST built by Robert Stephenson & Hawthorns(builder's No. 7794 of 1953) was cold in the yard at Ollerton Colliery on a very cold 16th March 1969. A Hudswell Clarke diesel stands behind.
*Horace Gamble/Transport Library*

**LEFT:** The Great Central design 30-lever Ollerton Colliery signal box on Wednesday 2nd April 2003. This box dated from 1926 and was equipped with a switch panel to control the Boughton area in 1984
*From a colour slide by Stephen Chapman*

**RIGHT:** The railway at Ollerton looking east on 2nd April 2003. The colliery complex has been razed and the ground landscaped. Only the two running lines remain, rusty and unused since the closure of High Marnham power station. Ollerton Colliery box stands defiant, guarded against misfortune by its signals. *From a colour slide by Stephen Chapman*

ABOVE: With scorched smokebox door, K2 2-6-0 No. 61780 heads the 2.12pm Skegness-Basford North into Ollerton at 4.21pm on Saturday 22nd August 1959. Empty stock is stabled behind the station, probably to form one of the local connecting services. *David Holmes*

LEFT: A somersault signal protects the line at the east end of Ollerton station while the staff turn out for this early 20th century photograph.

The goods depot on the right was listed in 1956 as having a 3-ton crane and equipped to handle general goods, livestock, furniture vans, carriages, motor cars, portable engines and machines on wheels. Ollerton closed to goods on 30th December 1968.

The station lost its regular passenger service when the Mansfield service was withdrawn on 19th September 1955 but remained open for miscellaneous traffic and parcels as well as summer Saturday services until 1964. *Railway Station Photographs*

ABOVE: No. 56018, one of the BR Class 56s built in Romania, passes 30-lever Thoresby Colliery GC 1926 signal box with empty MGR hoppers from High Marnham power station at 14.30 on Thursday 6th March 2003. The photographer was informed by the signalman that this was the return working of the very last MGR to the power station. The colliery branch is on the far left. *From a Stephen Chapman colour slide*

# TUXFORD-LANGWITH COLLIERY SIDINGS
*BRITISH RAILWAYS EASTERN REGION(SOUTHERN AREA) SECTIONAL APPENDIX JANUARY 1969*

**SIGNALLING:** Absolute Block Tuxford-Langwith Colliery Sidings(situated on the New Langwith curve.) One Engine in Steam: Langwith Colliery branch.

**MAXIMUM SPEED: On Main Lines:** 50mph. Langwith Junction-Colliery Sidings: 20mph. Langwith Colliery branch: 5mph.

**LOOPS AND REFUGE SIDINGS:** Down Refuge Siding at Tuxford West with standage for 68 wagons, engine and brake van; Up Refuge Siding at Tuxford Central with standage for 28 wagons, engine and brake van. Down Refuge Siding at Ollerton with standage for 61 wagons, engine and brake van; Up Refuge Siding at Ollerton with standage for 32 wagons, engine and brake van. Up Refuge Siding at Edwinstowe with standage for 54 wagons, engine and brake van.

**SIGNAL BOXES**(with distance from previous box): Tuxford West(3 miles 69 yds from High Marnham, Tuxford Station(1254yds,) Boughton Junction(3 miles 1168yds.,) Ollerton Colliery(1368yds.,) Ollerton Station(1 mile 440yds.,) Thoresby Colliery(1605yds.,) Edwinstowe(1293yds.,) Clipstone East Junction(1 mile 102yds.,) Clipstone West Junction(220yds.,) Welbeck Colliery Junction(2 miles 85yds.,) Warsop(1713yds.,) Langwith Junction(1561yds.,) Langwith Colliery Junction(1 mile 1432yds,) Langwith Colliery Sidings(640yds.)

**The Bevercotes Colliery branch** was worked according to One Engine in Steam rules with a maximum line speed of 30mph.

**The Thoresby Colliery branch** was worked according to One Engine in Steam rules with a maximum line speed of 15mph.

**The Thoresby Colliery branch** consisting of two single lines known as the "Loaded" and "Empty" sidings, each worked in accordance with "One Engine in Steam" regulations, commences at the one-lever ground frame at the junction of the two sidings... Two Train Staffs are provided in separate boxes at the ground frame...An indicator is provided in Thoresby Colliery box to show which Train Staff is "out."
*BR Eastern Region Sectional Appendix 1969*

**RIGHT:** Well cared for Peckett 0-4-0ST *Tophard* (builder's No. 1791 of 1932) at Thoresby Colliery on 15th May 1965. The aerial ropeway was a feature of many mining areas, another fascinating sight now extinct. Thoresby closed in 2015.
*Horace Gamble/Transport Library*

**LEFT:** LD&EC daily passenger ceased in 1955 but local trains still ran on summer Saturdays providing connections for intermediate stations with holiday expresses. Here, the 4.34pm Ollerton-Shirebrook North headed by J11 0-6-0 No. 64314 is seen west of Edwinstowe on Saturday 20th August 1960. The third track just visible on the left is the Edwinstowe Up refuge siding while the distant arms on the signal are for Clipstone East Junction.

**BELOW:** K3 2-6-0 No. 61912 passes Edwinstowe station with a westbound class 4 freight consisting of just four wagons and the guards van at 3.2pm on 26th August 1961. Notice how beautifully maintained the station is despite losing its regular passenger services six years ago. *This and picture above by David Holmes*

ABOVE: Staveley-based K3 2-6-0 No. 61976 passes Edwinstowe signal box as it enters the station with the 2.38pm Saturdays Only Shirebrook North-Ollerton at 2.56pm on 26th August 1961. The regular summer Saturday services such as this continued to serve Ollerton, Edwinstowe and Warsop stations until 5th September 1964. *David Holmes*
Goods facilities listed here in 1956 were the same as those at Ollerton while the passenger station handled parcels and miscellaneous traffic. There was also the Duke of Portland's public siding.

BELOW: Another of the special trains to be seen here, literally day-in day-out hence the epithet "DIDO" was the one-coach shuttle conveying staff between Tuxford and Langwith Junction. K3 No. 61958 is seen at Edwinstowe while taking the empty coach to Langwith Junction at 4.3pm on 26th August 1961. *David Holmes*

OPPOSITE: Substantial station buildings were provided at Edwinstowe by the LD&EC in the expectation that tourists would flock there to explore Sherwood Forest. The hordes didn't really materialise but the buildings survived the end of passenger traffic and this was them on Thursday 6th March 2003. *From a colour slide by Stephen Chapman*

| LD&EC LINE BOOKED SUMMER SATURDAY EXPRESS PASSENGER SERVICES 1963 ||
| --- | --- |
| 1E30 6.25am Radford-Skegness | 1M30 9.27 Skegness-Manchester Piccadilly |
| 1E31 6.40am Radford-Mablethorpe | 1M78 11.24 Mablethorpe-Radford |
| 1K24 8.26am Sheffield Victoria-Skegness | 1M73 12.44pm Skegness-Manchester Piccadilly |
| 1N42 8.33am Nottingham Midland-Scarborough Londesborough Rd. | 1M74 11.15am Yarmouth Vauxhall-Manchester Piccadilly |
| 1E33 8.27am Manchester Piccadilly-Skegness | 1M84 2pm Skegness-Radford |
| 1E32 9.45am Manchester Piccadilly-Yarmouth Vauxhall | 1M82 2.35pm Scarborough Londesborough Rd.-Nottingham Midland |

ABOVE: EWS General Motors Type 5 No. 66179 heads a train of empties along the Welbeck Colliery branch at 15.00 on Thursday 20th March 2003. *From a colour slide by Stephen Chapman* The Welbeck Colliery branch was worked in accordance with One Engine in Steam regulations with a maximum line speed of 15mph, raised to 25mph in 1980. In summer 1963 trip working 8T38 was booked to depart Welbeck Colliery Junction with empties at 7.28, 9.20 and 11.20am, returning from Welbeck Colliery with fulls at 8.30 and 10.30am and 12.30 and 8.5pm. The latter two ran to Shirebrook Sidings. Trip 8T39 worked between Welbeck Colliery Junction and Mansfield Concentration Sidings. Welbeck Colliery closed in 2011.

RIGHT: Clipstone Junction(previously Clipstone West) signal box on Monday 17th March 2003. The box was situated in the fork between the main line and the Clipstone West-South curve. A Great Central box dating from 1917 it had 37 levers and was equipped in 1986 with an entrance-exit(NX) panel for the Rufford Junction area. *From a colour slide by Stephen Chapman.*

**ABOVE: WD 2-8-0 No. 90418 with a long train of 21-ton hopper wagons at Clipstone West Junction in the early 1960s. The signal is off for the train to proceed round the curve to Mansfield Concentration Sidings. The apparent lack of movement and personnel on the track is because this was a test run organized to assess brake block wear on the locomotive.** *Tom Greaves*

*At 7.36am on 12th May 1950 the* 7.25am Shirebrook North to Lincoln passenger train consisting of three coaches hauled by N5 0-6-2T No. 69319 was derailed between Clipstone West and East junctions. The whole of the train was derailed but no-one was seriously injured. About 170 yards of track were destroyed, blocking both lines between West and East Junctions. Both junctions were clear and so trains were diverted via Clipstone South Junction.

Following a public inquiry, the Ministry of Transport inspecting officer Colonel R. J. Walker concluded that the derailment was caused by the condition of the track, particularly excessive reversals in the cross-level causing the engine to oscillate, and to a degree the condition of 69319 which was found to have five of its eight coil springs broken, three known to be broken before the derailment, despite having undergone a general repair in March 1949. The track was due for renewal the following month.

Col. Walker's report stated: "It[the train] had just passed through the junction facing points running at about 35mph with the regulator closed on the falling gradient, when it became completely derailed on the plain line beyond." The report also stated that the train ran along the ballast for 178 yards and veered across to the Down line and back to the Up line. The body of the third coach(E51631) became detached from its bogies and fell over on its side.

The report described the line as "classified as a 'Primary B line; its traffic is mainly freight. From Shirebrook North it rises for about 3 1/2 miles to Welbeck Colliery, runs level for half a mile, and then falls for nearly 1 1/4 miles at 1 in 100 to Clipstone West Junction."

**ABOVE: A Class A5 4-6-2T rolls into Warsop station with a Lincoln-Shirebrook North service in the early 1950s. Just beyond here on the right was the Stanton Iron & Chemcial Co.'s sand quarry which was served by a short industrial branch.** *Railway Station Photographs*

**ABOVE:** Looking west towards Langwith Junction as Class O4/8 2-8-0 No. 63731 approaches Warsop Junction Up Sidings with a coal trip at 1.17pm on 13th October 1962. Just beyond the signals is the bridge carrying the LD&EC over the former Midland Shireoaks-Mansfield line while the back end of the train has just passed through Shirebrook North station. The curve from the Midland line at Shirebrook Junction used to come in from the left. In more recent times the line here was redirected through a new cutting in the field on the right to a north facing junction on the Midland line, thus wiping Langwith Junction from the national network. *Robert Anderson*

**LEFT:** At 1.10pm on a truly dismal 3rd December 1960, J11 0-6-0 No. 64333 is about to pass Warsop Junction Sidings with the "DIDO" to Tuxford. That's not Shirebrook Cathedral but Langwith Junction coaling plant standing tall above the engine shed which looks very much in need of roof repairs. *The late John Beaumont/Robert Anderson collection*

**LANGWITH JUNCTION.** Trains proceeding into the Warsop Junction reception lines from the direction of Shirebrook North, must not exceed 39 wagons, and Guards must see that the rear of the train is inside the reception line clear of adjoining lines. When it is necessary for an engine to return by Nos.1 and 2 reception lines for the purposes of attaching the brake van, the Guard must communicate with the signalman at Langwith Junction by telephone, and the engine must run forward to the four-arm bracket signal to allow the signalman to operate the motors, before he is able to back on to his brake van. When drivers are assisting in the rear of trains from Nos. 1 and 2 reception lines in the direction of Shirebrook North, the assisting engine must stop as soon as it arrives inside the four arm bracket signal until the signal is lowered for it to return to the reception line. *BR Eastern Region Sectional Appendix January 1969*

ABOVE: Passing under the bridge from which the previous scenes were captured, four 2-8-0s, their duties fulfiled, make their way light engine from Mansfield Concentration Sidings to Langwith Junction shed at 1.35pm on 13th October 1962. The engines are, from front: O4s Nos. 63842 and 63801, and WDs Nos. 90460 and 90449. *Robert Anderson*

**LANGWITH JUNCTION-CLIPSTONE LIGHT ENGINE MOVEMENTS 6AM - 8AM SUMMER 1963**

| | | |
|---|---|---|
| 5.55 MX | 0E00 | 5.50 Langwith Jn. Loco-Mansfield Central  *Station pilot* |
| 6.1 | 8M83 | 8.30pmSO/4.35amMX Sheffield Bernard Rd.-Mansfield Central |
| 6.10 | 0M23 | 6.5 Langwith Jn. Loco-Warsop Junction.  *To work 6.50 Mottram* |
| 6.14 MX | 7E67 | 12.15 Halewood-Whitemoor |
| 6.17 MO | 0M50 | 6.10 Langwith Jn. Loco-Mansfield Conc. Sidings  *To work 7.33 Annesley*\* |
| 6.17 MO | 0T48 | 6.10 Langwith Jn. Loco-Mansfield Conc. Sidings engine & brake van\* |
| 6.17 MO | 0E96 | 6.10 Langwith Jn. Loco-Mansfield Conc. Sidings  *To work 7.10 Colwick*\* |
| 6.24 MO | 0 | 6.19 Langwith Jn. Loco-Mansfield Conc. Sidings  *Mansfield Concentration Sidings pilot*\* |
| 6.24 MO | 0T36 | 6.19 Langwith Jn. Loco-Warsop Main Colliery \* |
| 6.24 MO | 0E00 | 6.19 Langwith Jn.-Mansfield Central  *Station pilot*\* |
| 6.40 | 0 | 6.30 Langwith Jn. Loco-Warsop Junction 2 engines. One to work 7.15 Sheffield Bernard Road |
| 6.40 | 0T40 | 6.35 Langwith Jn.-Mansfield Conc. Sidings\* |
| 6.40 | 0T43 | 6.35 Langwith Jn.-Mansfield Conc. Sidings\* |
| 6.47 | 0T38 | 6.40 Langwith Jn .Loco-Welbeck Colliery Jn. Engine and brake van |
| 6.55 | 0T41 | 6.50 Langwith Jn. Loco-Mansfield Colliery |
| 7.5 | 0T47 | 7.0 Langwith Jn. Loco-Ollerton Colliery  *Ollerton pilot* |
| 7.16 | 0T44 | 7.10 Langwith Jn. Loco-Mansfield Conc. Sidings engine and brake van |
| 7.20 | 0M51 | 7.15 Langwith Jn. Loco-Warsop Jn. To work *7.52 Annesley* |
| 7.27 | 0T45 | 7.20 Langwith Jn. Loco-Thoresby Colliery Jn.  Engine and brake van |
| 8.10 | 0T46 | 8.5 Langwith Jn. Loco.-Bevercotes Colliery |

\**Engines shown off the shed at the same times are of course running coupled together*

**LANGWITH JUNCTION DOWN YARD.** When it is necessary for a BR movement to be made into Langwith Junction Down Yard the person in charge of the movement must instruct Messrs. W. H. Davies & Sons staff to stand their locomotive clear in the group of sidings 3 to 6 until the BR movement has been withdrawn from the sidings. *BR Eastern Region Sectional Appendix 1969*

Being situated at an important junction at the heart of the coalfield, Langwith Junction eclipsed Tuxford as the main provider of engines for the LD&EC lines and beyond. As built, it consisted of a two road shed with a northlight roof but as the depot expanded further sheds with ordinary pitched roofs were added. It began the BR era coded 40E in the Lincoln District, but administrative changes in 1958 saw it transferred to the Sheffield Division when it was given the code 41J which it held for the rest of its time. It was primarily a freight depot providing engines for the many mineral workings of the area and its allocation consisted mainly of 2-8-0s and 0-6-0s and, later, Class 9F 2-10-0s. It also had a small selection of tank engines for shunting and local passenger work. In October 1965 its allocation was increased with engines transferred from Barrow Hill which had closed to steam, though some were on paper only. The depot closed completely in February 1966 after which the 41J code was switched to the new diesel depot at neighbouring Shirebrook West. Part of the shed buildings were taken over and incorporated into the wagon works of W. H. Davies Ltd.

ABOVE: A view at the north end of Langwith Junction depot in the 1950s with various engines on show. On the left are ex-Army Railway Operating Division O4/3 2-8-0 No. 63840, a B1 4-6-0 and a K3 2-6-0, in the centre a WD 2-8-0 and on the right a J11 0-6-0, behind which is a tank engine. The original two-road shed is on the right and the later three-road shed further back on the left. *Colour-Rail*

ABOVE: In 1907 Langwith Junction shed became part of the Great Central Railway along with the rest of the LD&EC and in common with most GC sheds it had outdoor sheerlegs to assist with repairs. One has to sympathise with the fitters who had to work on engines outdoors in all weathers but then they were tough in those days. Class O4/7 2-8-0 No. 63634 is on the sheerlegs road with a WD 2-8-0 on 2nd June 1957. *Stephen Chapman archive*

**LOCOMOTIVES ALLOCATED TO LANGWITH JUNCTION**
**AUGUST 1950:** O4 2-8-0: 63577/85/97/615/25/32/44/8/56/8/65/6/77/9/83/703/7/9/15/7/24/41/50/7/8/9/65/76/800/7/9/33/7/40/2/70/84/900/2; J11 0-6-0: 64281/9/97/310/21/58/78/9/89/414/8/26/7; N5 0-6-2T: 69284/319/23/7; A5 4-6-2T: 69812/5/81; Q1 0-8-0T: 69928/9: **Total: 61.**
**SUMMER 1963:** O4 2-8-0: 63577/615/36/79/83/91/7/703/15/7/20/32/9/63/5/800/28/9/42/53/61/93/902; WD 2-8-0: 90003/43/88/145/209/24/75/301/2/411/8/42/9/83; 350hp 0-6-0 diesel: D3325/701/4053/7/60/1/6/7/9/85. **Total: 47.**
*Steam breakdown crane No.101 with a 15-ton capacity and of Route Availability 3 was allocated to Langwith Junction with the Instruction that it must not work over any former Great Eastern routes.*

**LANGWITH JUNCTION MPD BOOKED PILOT DUTIES SUMMER 1963**
**Langwith Jn.** 6am-10pm Monday-Saturday    Marshals as required
**Mansfield Concentration Sidings No.1**    6.45am Monday-12.30am Sunday    Shunts Yard
**Mansfield Concentration Sidings No. 2**    9am Monday-10pm Saturday    Shunts Yard
**Mansfield Central Station**    7.5am-6.30pm Monday, 6.25am -6.35pm Tuesday-Friday, 6.25am-2.50pm Saturday
**Warsop Jn. No.1**    6am Monday-Friday - 2am Tuesday-Saturday, 6.25am-10pm Saturday    Up Side
**Warsop Jn. No.2**    9am Monday-Friday - 6am Tuesday-Friday, 9am-10pm Saturday    Down Side

**ABOVE:** A view at the south end of the depot in the 1930s with a foreigner present in the shape of LNER J28 0-6-0 No. 2420, formerly of the Hull & Barnsley Railway. *Neville Stead collection/Transport Library*

**RIGHT:** Langwith Junction shed yard on 2nd May 1979 by which time it had become part of the W. H. Davies wagon works. The firm's shunter at that time was ex-army Ruston & Hornsby 4-wheel diesel 224347 of 1945. *Adrian Booth*

**ABOVE: Further shed rebuilding and expansion had taken place by the time of this early 1960s view of stalwart WD No. 90418 basking in the sun between the old and new sheds.** *Tom Greaves*

**BELOW: One of the engines allocated to Langwith Junction for local passenger duty, A5 4-6-2T No. 69828 rests in the yard on 14th August 1955. It had previously been allocated to Neasden for london suburban services.** *Stephen Chapman archive*

**RIGHT: One of the Q1 0-8-0 tanks designed for heavy shunting work, No. 69928, on shed with a K3 2-6-0 in the 1950s. These engines were rebuilt from ex-Great Central Q4 tender engines during the 1940s.
The turntable in the foreground looks to be under repair.** *Stephen Chapman archive*

**LEFT: Visiting the shed during summer Saturday passenger duty at 3.50pm on 15th August 1959 was D11 4-4-0 No. 62668 *Jutland*.** *David Holmes,*

ABOVE: Langwith Junction was where the Leen Valley Extension line met the LD&EC, thus providing an alternative through route for the GC main line between Kirkby South Junction and Killamarsh, a route which was certainly no by-way. In dismal weather at 12.17pm on 3rd December 1960, Doncaster B1 4-6-0 No. 61157 sets out with the 12.15pm Shirebrook North-Leicester class A excursion, passing Langwith Junction shed on its way towards the GC main line via Pleasley and Sutton-in-Ashfield.
*The late John Beaumont/Robert Anderson collection*

BELOW: When the Leen Valley Extension was opened the Great Northern ran a passenger service between Nottingham and Shirebrook South only which was extended to Shirebrook North by the LNER so that it could connect with other services. Here, Stirling 0-4-4T No. 242 has arrived at Shirebrook South with a service from Nottingham. *Railway Station Photographs*

**ABOVE: Travelling south from Shirebrook, the line passed through Pleasley and then Skegby(Skegby for Stanton Hill) station which is pictured here looking towards Langwith Junction.** *Railway Station Photographs*

**BELOW: As with the LD&EC, although having lost its daily year-round passenger service as long ago as September 1931 - Sutton in Ashfield Town was temporarily reopened 20th February to 17th September 1956 - the Leen Valley Extension stations were maintained for excursions and summer Saturdays, and an advertised summer Saturday service was provided. Here, B1 4-6-0 No. 61152 leaves Sutton-in-Ashfield Town with the 5.24pm Nottingham Victoria-Shirebrook North stopping service at 5.57 on 22nd August 1959.** *David Holmes* **The goods yard on the right was listed in 1956 as having a 1 1/2-ton permanent crane and able to handle all kinds of traffic. A private siding served served the Metal Box Company. Goods facilities were withdrawn in February 1965.**

**The portion of the Leen Valley Extension** line from Langwith Junction to the boundary with the London Midland Region at Pleasley East was shown in the BR Eastern Region Sectional Appendix January 1969 as worked by Absolute Block signalling with a maximum line speed of 40mph. Pleasley Colliery signal box was 3miles 983yds from Shirebrook North. Although freight only by this time, the line was listed in Table K2 of the Appendix as being equipped for use by passenger trains. The line ceased to exist when it was deleted from the Sectional Appendix per a supplement issued on 4th May 1970.

ABOVE: Accelerating into Shirebrook North from the Leen Valley direction at 11.5am on 10th November 1962 with an express freight, thought to be 4N24 the 7.35am Woodford to York, is 14A Cricklewood-allocated BR Standard Class 4 2-6-0 No. 76036. In the distance, the signal is off for a train going towards Clipstone while what appears to be an O4 2-8-0 waits for 76036 to clear before proceeding towards Shirebrook. The station used to have an elegant lattice footbridge but by the time of this picture it had been replaced by the more functional plate girder version seen here - but the old gas lamps survive. *Robert Anderson.*

BELOW: It's early spring and J11 0-6-0 No. 64427 is waiting to leave with a service to Lincoln. The line to Chesterfield stretches away behind the train and, judging from close inspection, buffer stops have already been erected following the line's closure which will date this picture between 1951 and 1955. *Neville Stead collection/Transport Library*

**ABOVE: A rocky outcrop between the Chesterfield and Killamarsh lines provides the ideal vantage point for this panoramic view of Shirebrook North station's west end. The occasion bringing out the crowds this time is a Stephenson Locomotive Society railtour headed by Ivatt Class 2 2-6-0 No. 46443 on 3rd July 1954.** *From a Colour-Rail colour slide*

**BELOW: In decidedly ropy external condition is D11 4-4-0 No. 62669** *Ypres* **at Shirebrook North with the summer Saturday 4.18pm from Ollerton at 5.20 on 15th August 1959. The state of the engine hardly presents a good image of rail travel for all those who probably only use it once a year. And no doubt the coaching stock will be little better. David Holmes, who took the photo, commented: "I have never seen a loco in such appaling condition actually in traffic. Obviously** *Ypres* **had been kept in store all winter in order to work a few summer trains like this."**

LEFT: J11 No. 64379 shunts the goods yard at Shirebrook North at 5.17pm on 20th August 1960. *David Holmes*
Goods facilities included a 3-ton permanent crane, just visible in front of the building on the left. Shirebrook North was listed in 1956 as equipped to handle all types of freight except horse boxes and prize cattle vans, and carriage trucks and motor cars by passenger or parcels train. The goods shed is on the right, immediately behind the coach which will no doubt attract the eye of coaching stock experts. Goods facilities were withdrawn with effect from 4th January 1965.

**Leen valley advertised passenger service 12th June-10th September 1961**
**Saturdays Only**
*Shirebrook North times*
**am**
**6.0** Though carriages to Skegness calling at Shirebrook South, Pleasley East, Sutton-in-Ashfield Town, Hucknall Central, Bulwell Common Nottingham Victoria.
*1st July-19th August*

**pm**
**1.25** to Nottingham Victoria calling at the same stations.
**1.57** 1.5 from Nottingham Victoria calling at Hucknall Central, Sutton-in-Ashfield Town, Pleasley East, Shirebrook South. Through carriages from Skegness.
*1st July-19th August.*
**5.25 f**rom Nottingham Victoria all stations except New Basford.

ABOVE: Performing Saturday coaching stock pilot duty at Shirebrook North at 5.7pm on 20th August 1960 was N5 0-6-2T No. 69263. *David Holmes*

ABOVE: This view looking down from the footbridge shows the arrangement of lines at Shirebrook North. The former Chesterfield line goes straight ahead and the line to Killamarsh via Spink Hill to the right. The station, named Langwith Junction until June 1924, was closed to regular passenger services from 19th September 1955 but continued to handle parcels and miscellaneous traffic. It was maintained in good order for excursions and the summer Saturday services advertised in the public timetable which continued to run until 5th September 1964. *Railway Station Photographs*

BELOW: Back to business as usual and away from the relative glamour of dirty Directors is O4/8 2-8-0 No. 63801 pounding through the station with a Through Freight composed of mineral wagons for the Spink Hill line at 5.36pm on 26th August 1961. *David Holmes*

**ABOVE:** Coming the other way, pounding hard up the 1 in 120 into Shirebrook North off the Spink Hill line at 11.40am on a dark and murky 10th November 1962, is O4/8 No. 63679 with a 1000-ton class 7 unfitted express freight. The train is possibly the 5.40am Heaton Mersey to Warsop Junction empties which 63679 will have worked from Rotherwood having taken over from electric traction. *Robert Anderson*

**BELOW:** Clowne South station looking towards Spink Hill while receiving an invasion of gricers. The station closed to regular passengers as long ago as 10th September 1939 when the Sheffield Midland-Mansfield Town service was withdrawn. The goods depot, seen on the left remained in business until 4th July 1960. It was listed in 1956 as equipped to handle all classes of freight while the crane, visible behind the fence, was of 3 ton capacity. *Railway Station Photographs.*

**ABOVE:** Back to summer Saturday traffic and K3 2-6-0 No. 61948, of 31B March shed, runs into Clowne South with the 8.51am additional service from Great Yarmouth to Castleton at 2.9pm on 26th August 1961. *David Holmes*

**BELOW:** Clowne Station signal box with wagons occupying the adjacent sidings on 24th July 1960. Out of view behind the wagons in the sidings on the left is the former Midland Elmton & Creswell to Staveley line which outlived the Spink Hill line by 30 years or more. Going west, this line will shortly pass over the Midland and head north towards Spink Hill.

*Alec Swain/ Transport Treasury*

**Spink Hill line booked Saturday passenger services Summer 1963:**
**am**
8.26 Sheffield-Victoria to Skegness
8.37 Manchester Piccadilly to Skegness
9.45 Manchester Piccadilly to Yarmouth
9.27 Skegness-Manchester Piccadilly
11.15 Yarmouth Vauxhall-Manchester Piccadilly
**pm**
12.44 Skegness-Manchester Piccadilly
2.0 Scarborough-Nottingham Midland *runs when required.*

LEFT: Near Spink Hill an unidentified express headed by Britannia Pacific No. 70005 *John Milton* climbs through the murk towards Clowne and Langwith Junction. The Langwith Junction-Killamarsh line was shown as no longer available for passenger trains in a supplement to the Sectional Appendix issued on 4th May 1970. *J. Langford/Photos from the Fifties*

BELOW: Spink Hill station looking towards Spink Hill Tunnel which is just beyond the overbridge. The picture is undated but the line might have been closed beyond here by this time. The station looks to be a private residence while wagons appear to be stored on the Up line. Wagons visible behind the station are probably for Westthorpe Colliery. *Railway Station Photographs.*
Spink Hill station itself closed to passengers on 10th September 1939 and to goods on 4th January 1965. Goods facilities were listed in 1956 as having a 3-ton capacity permanent crane and equipped to handle all classes of freight.

RIGHT: In steam days, the NCB locomotive fleet at Westthorpe Colliery included Austerity 0-6-0 saddle tanks acquired from the War Department which retained their WD numbers. This is No. 75034 built by Hunslet Engine Co. of Leeds in 1943, builders No. 2883, on 8th March 1964. Also there was No. 75127, Hunslet 3177 of 1944.
*Alec Swain/Transport Treasury*

**RIGHT: In the diesel era, Westthorpe had these two big diesel hydraulic 0-6-0s built by the Yorkshire Engine Co. at Meadowhall in 1963. They are builders Nos. 2910 (previously at Markham Colliery, Duckmanton) and 2911 which are seen at Westthorpe on 2nd May 1979.** *From a colour slide by Adrian Booth*

**ABOVE: Coming away from Killamarsh Junction the Spink Hill line rose sharply through a winding sandstone cutting. Class O4/8 2-8-0 No. 63679 wheezes its way up the gradient with a heavy load of empties at 6.20pm on 26th May 1962.** *Robert Anderson*

### Updates and amendments

Page 80: Mr. J. Longford writes to add that the train from which he took to photo on 31st October 1959 is the Liverpool-Harwich boat train, diverted via Spink Hill and the LD&EC due to a lorry hitting a bridge at Waleswood.

Page 85 middle: The wrong location was supplied with this picture. It is not Clipstone Colliery but Clifton Colliery, Nottingham.

Page 107 bottom: The date of this picture should read 16th March 1968 which more readily explains the full yellow end on the DMU.

Upon closu... Beighton Ju... The 1969 B... Absolute Bl... Junction,) a... was from B... Killamarsh ... Train Work... 4th May 19... Westthorpe... might be u... a run-rou...

...nction line, a three mile section from ...horpe Colliery. ...d it as being double line worked by ...unction (1 mile 71yds from Beighton ...amarsh Central Jn.) The Up direction ...peed was 30mph. The gradient from ...d to single track operated under "One ...l according to a supplement issued on ...k was abandoned despite hopes that it ...on was retained at the Beighton end as

**ABOVE: At 2.25pm on 24th November 1962 B1 4-6-0 No. 61041 is seen climbing away from Killamarsh Junction with the 2.10pm Staveley-Langwith Junction freight, 61041 having run round its train at Killamarsh Junction.** *Robert Anderson*

**BELOW: Just a cobbles throw from the remains of King John's hunting palace, Mansfield Concentration Sidings, sometimes referred to as Clipstone Sidings, were the hub for coal and other freight operations in the Sherwood area, being centrally located for all the big new collieries served by the Mansfield Railway and the LD&EC. Here, a pair of Class 08 shunters are parked alongside Concentration Sidings signal box in August 1980.** *Malcolm Roughley/Stephen Chapman archive*

# THE MANSFIELD RAILWAY

**ABOVE: An August 1980 view which reveals the extent of Mansfield Concentration Sidings. The Down yard is on the left and the Up behind the Class 56. As can be seen, the traffic here is still in conventional mineral wagons although an MGR hopper can be glimpsed in the Up yard.** *Malcolm Roughley/Stephen Chapman archive*

**BELOW: Early 1960s steam action at Mansfield Concentration Sidings. Relatively clean Class O4/8 2-8-0 No. 63828 starts a hefty class 8 coal train, most likely destined for Annesley, out of the Up yard. An 8F 2-8-0 waits with a brake van and another O4 stands further back in the yard.** *Tom Greaves*

**ABOVE: Shunting operations under way in the Down yard, August 1980.** *Malcolm Roughley/Stephen Chapman archive*

**BELOW: A pair of O4s, O4/8 63731 leading with a brake van, have arrived from Langwith Junction to take up their duties. In the background another O4 takes water while an 8F 2-8-0 waits for the road.** *Tom Greaves*

**The January 1969 Eastern Region Sectional Appendix listed the Mansfield Railway** from the London Midland Region boundary at Mansfield Central to Clipstone as signalled by Absolute Block. The maximum line speed was 30mph from Mansfield Colliery but only 15mph from the boundary to Mansfield Colliery. Additional running lines were Up and Down Goods signalled by Permissive Bock from Rufford Junction to Concentrations Sidings. Signal boxes(with distance from previous box) were Mansfield Colliery(2 miles 1248yds from Mansfield Central box,) Rufford Jn.(1 mile 303yds,) Concentration Sidings(1277yds,) Clipstone West Jn.(1 mile,) and Clipstone East Jn. 220yds.)

ABOVE: Looking from Mansfield Concentration Sidings in the direction of Rufford Junction in August 1980. *Malcolm Roughley/ Stephen Chapman archive*

Upon the complete end of coal mining by the early 21st century, everything south of Clipstone junctions, including Concentration Sidings and the colliery branches, was closed and lifted.

First of the pits going south on the Mansfield Railway was Clipstone itself, noted for hiring or borrowing engines from BR to do its internal shunting.

CENTRE: Original Midland Railway "Jinty" 3F 0-6-0T No. 47231, of Toton shed, has rather oddly acquired the chimney from a J11, possibly to improve clearances. *From a Colour-Rail colour slide*

BOTTOM: In this scene on 23rd April 1960 J94 0-6-0ST No. 68080 - the last in the class - has been borrowed from Langwith Junction. *Alec Swain/ Transport Treasury*

Clipstone Colliery was served by both Mansfield Railway and Midland branches. The Midland reached the colliery by a single line from Rufford Colliery worked by One Engine in Steam using a triangular red staff as authority for the driver to proceed.

RIGHT: One of Clipstone's own locos was this mighty Yorkshire Engine Co. Workhorse class 0-6-0ST, builders No. 2521 of 1952, pictured on 16th March 1969. Clipstone Colliery closed in 2003. *Horace Gamble/Transport Library*

**Booked colliery Trips Summer 1963**
**From Mansfield Concentration Sidings**
am
7.13   8T43 Bilsthorpe
7.20   8T40 Rufford
8.35   8T44 Clipstone
8.45   9M60 Blidworth
9.48   8T44 Clipstone
10.48  8T43 Bilsthorpe
11.00  8T40 Rufford
11.15  8T41 Mansfield
pm
12.25  9M61 Blidworth
2.15   8T43 Bilsthorpe
2.25   8T40 Rufford
2.30   8T40 Rufford
2.45   8T41 Mansfield
3.50   8T44 Clipstone
5.40   8T43 Bilsthorpe
5.55   9T41 Mansfield

LEFT: Looking north to Rufford Junction on 19th March 2003 by which time the track had been considerably slimmed down and the signalling modernized. Centre left is Clipstone Colliery Junction and the single line to the colliery which was about to close. The 1969 BR Sectional Appendix showed this short branch as worked according to One Engine in Steam rules with a 15mph maximum speed.
The 40mph speed limit for the colliery branch to Rufford on the right is impressive. Not far behind the photographer was the junction with the Blidworth Colliery branch, by this time lifted beyond the junction with the branch to Bilsthorpe Colliery. The line on the left had previously continued to Mansfield. *Stephen Chapman*

RIGHT: **Disappearing through the woodlands the disused Bilsthorpe Colliery branch evokes the atmosphere of a German Iron Curtain frontier line during the Cold War. This view on 19th March 2003 is towards Bilsthorpe where the colliery closed in 1997.** *From a Stephen Chapman colour slide.* **The woods, incidentally, are much more benign, being part of the Sherwood Pines Forest Park.**

**The Rufford Colliery branch** was shown by the BR 1969 Sectional Appendix as worked by electric token with key Token instruments at Bilsthorpe Colliery Jn.(1 mile 396yds from Rufford Jn.) and Blidworth Colliery Jn.(484yds from Bilsthorpe Jn.) The maximum speed allowed then was 15mph.

**Clearance of loads from Rufford No.2 stocking site(at ground frame on Bilsthorpe Junction-Bilsthorpe Colliery single line.)** A train consisting of 2 locos and brake van may be allowed to proceed from Rufford Junction to Bilsthorpe Junction Key Token station and thence to Bilsthorpe Colliery ground frame for the purpose of clearing loaded wagons from the stocking site.. On arrival at the stocking site the trailing loco may be uncoupled. The other loco will then be responsible for drawing the wagons out of the stocking site and placing them on the loco which has been uncoupled......

*BR Eastern Region Sectional Appendix January 1969*

BELOW: **Bilsthorpe Colliery on 15th May 1965 when this Smith & Rodley steam grab appeared to be engaged in some general cleaning up work.**
*Horace Gamble/Transport Library*

87

ABOVE: Gricers pay homage to Bilsthorpe Colliery's loco fleet on 15th May 1965. The two 0-6-0STs are Andrew Barclay 2077, built 1939(left) and Hawthorn Leslie 3614, built 1925.
*Horace Gamble/Transport Library*

LEFT: The end of the Rufford branch at Spring Hill as seen on 19th March 2003 amidst vegetation typical of the area. After Rufford Colliery closed in 1993, the line was kept alive until the early 21st century by the existence of a coal stacking ground, situated just beyond the scrub on the right, where surplus coal from other pits was stored until required. *From a Stephen Chapman colour slide*

RIGHT: Peckett 0-4-0ST 2092 of 1947 was doing the work at Mansfield (Crown Farm) Colliery on 15th May 1965. Mansfield Colliery closed in 1989.
*Horace Gamble/ Transport Library*

**ABOVE:** The scene on 2nd September 1950 after the 9.18am Nottingham-Edwinstowe had left the rails between Mansfield Central and Rufford Junction and plunged down an embankment at 35-40mph. Incredibly neither the three passengers or guard were hurt while the driver and fireman on N2 0-6-2T No. 69552, seen on its side down the bank, were described as having had a "lucky escape." The Great Central Mansfield Colliery branch and sidings are in the background. *Transport Treasury*

**BELOW:** In the early 1950s, A5 4-6-2T No. 69810 awaits departure from Mansfield Central's wooden platforms with a local service to Nottingham Victoria. *Neville Stead Collection/Transport Library* Mansfield Central(just plain Mansfield until 1950) closed to regular passenger services on 2nd January 1956 but continued to handle passengers on summer Saturdays when it could be rather busy as seen with the advertised departures for summer 1961: **5.53am**(5.30 Ollerton-Yarmouth;) **7.26**(6.40 Basford North-Skegness;) **7.36**(6.50 Basford North-Mablethorpe;) **8.48**(8.0 Nottingham Vic.-Cleethorpes;) **9.22**(7.50 Leicester Cen.-Scarborough;) **9.59**(9.15 Basford North-Scarborough;) **2.22pm**(11.30 Mablethorpe-Basford North;) **3.58** (1.28 Cleethorpes-Nottingham/to Leicester 5th, 12th & 19th Aug.;) **4.49**(2.12 Skegness-Basford North;) **6.18arr**( 5.35 from Nottingham Vic.;) **6.24**(2.35pm Scarborough-Basford North;) **7.15**(1.50 Yarmouth-Ollerton;) **7.32arr**(6.47 from Nottingham Vic.;) **11.50pm** Fridays Only to Nottingham Vic.

ABOVE: Class O1 2-8-0 No. 63886 heads a Clipstone Sidings-Annesley coal train away from Mansfield Central on 1st October 1959. It will shortly pass the goods depot and then pass under the Mansfield-Southwell line. *Tony Cooke/Colour-Rail*

BELOW: Langwith Junction's N5 0-6-2T No. 69299 was the Mansfield Central pilot on 10th October 1959. The goods yard here was quite extensive with plentiful traffic at this time. In 1956 goods facilities were listed as having a 7½-ton permanent crane(in 1938 the crane capacity was 10-tons) and the ability to handle general goods, livestock, and furniture vans, carriages, motor cars, portable engines and machines on wheels. Even so, we can see here that the yard crane has already been dismantled, in all probability replaced by a mobile crane. The line of vans on the right is deceptive as they are marked as condemned for scrapping. Mansfield Central closed to goods traffic with effect from 13th June 1966. The Mansfield Railway south of Mansfield Colliery was deleted from the Sectional Appendix per a supplement issued on 4th May 1970. *Tony Cooke/Colour-Rail*

ABOVE: Class J11 0-6-0 No. 64364 of Langwith Junction shed shunts Mansfield Central goods yard on 21st July 1959. *Tony Cooke/Colour-Rail.*

## SHIREOAKS-MANSFIELD

The railway from Shireoaks Junction to Mansfield had a completely different flavour to those covered so far - because it was a product of the Midland Railway with different architecture and locomotives originating from the Midland and its successor from 1923 the London Midland & Scottish Railway.
ABOVE: Leaving the former Great Central line at Shireoaks Junction, the first port of call on the way to Mansfield was Steetley Colliery and the quarries of the Steetley Manufacturing Co.'s ceramics division. This is Steetley Colliery on 28th August 1979. In the mid-1970s it had two ex-BR diesel mechanical locomotives for shunting - Class 04 No. D2328 and Class 05 No. D2607. The surface works shown here closed in 1983 when Steetley was combined with Shireoaks Colliery and coal wound there instead. *Adrian Booth*

# MANSFIELD WOODHOUSE-SHIREOAKS EAST JUNCTION
*BRITISH RAILWAYS EASTERN REGION(SOUTHERN AREA) SECTIONAL APPENDIX JANUARY 1969*

**SIGNALLING:** Absolute Block

**MAXIMUM SPEED: On Main Lines:** 60mph

**LOOPS AND REFUGE SIDINGS:** Down Refuge Siding at Shirebrook West with standage for 38 wagons, engine and brake van; Down Refuge Siding at Shirebrook Station with standage for 40 wagons, engine and brake van; Down Refuge Siding at Elmton & Creswell with standage for 42 wagons, engine and brake van.

**SIGNAL BOXES** (with distance from previous box): Shirebrook Sidings(1 mile 388yds from Mansfield Woodhouse box;) Shirebrook West Station(1578yds.;) Shirebrook Junction(320yds.;) Langwith Colliery(2miles 234yds.;) Elmton & Creswell(2 miles 278yds;) Whitwell(1 mile 191yds;) Steetley Colliery Sidings(1 mile 1452yds.;) Woodend Junction(1 mile 882yds.;) Shireoaks East Junction(900yds.)

**Private Sidings between Shireoaks and Mansfield Woodhouse as listed in the 1956 Handbook of Stations:** Steetley Lime Quarry, Shireoaks; Steetley Lime Works; Refractory Brick Co. Ltd. of England. *via Steetley Lime Works;* NCB Steetley Colliery; Capt. C.F.W. Jones Siding, *via Steetley Colliery;* G. Palmer, *via Steetley Colliery;* J. Warriner. *via Steetley Colliery;* NCB Whitwell Colliery; NCB Creswell Colliery; BR Norwood Public Siding; Sheepbridge Co. Ltd.; NCB Langwith Colliery; Peach & Co. Siding; NCB Welbeck Colliery & Brick Works; NCB Warsop Main Colliery & Lime Quarry; NCB Shirebrook Colliery; W.J.F. Sills' Lime Works; NCB Sherwood Colliery & Brick Works.

BELOW: Shunting at Steetley Lime Works, probably in the 1960s, is *June*, an 0-4-0ST built by the Yorkshire Engine Company in 1942, builders No. 2407.
*R. C. Riley/Transport Treasury.*

Years later, when steam was replaced by diesel the Yorkshire Engine Co. tradition was maintained when 0-4-0 diesel electric No 2652 of 1957 *Oughtibridge No.1* was used. The works had become part of the Oughtibridge Silica Firebrick Co. Ltd., hence the diesel's name

**On Sunday 18th June 1972** British Rail ran three 10-coach loco-hauled excursions from Elmton & Creswell to Cleethorpes on behalf of Whitwell Working Men's Club. The empty coaching stock came from Nunnery Carriage Sidings, Sheffield, via Shireoaks to Elmton & Creswell where each train ran round, being booked to depart at 07.14(1G07,) 07.58(1G08,) and 08.15(1G09.) They called at Whitwell 07.45-08.00, 08.03-15, 08.19-32 and ran to Cleethorpes via Retford, Gainsborough and Barnetby They were due to arrive back at Whitwell at 20.22, 21.05 and 21.31 before running round again at Elmton & Creswell and returning to Nunnery Sidings.

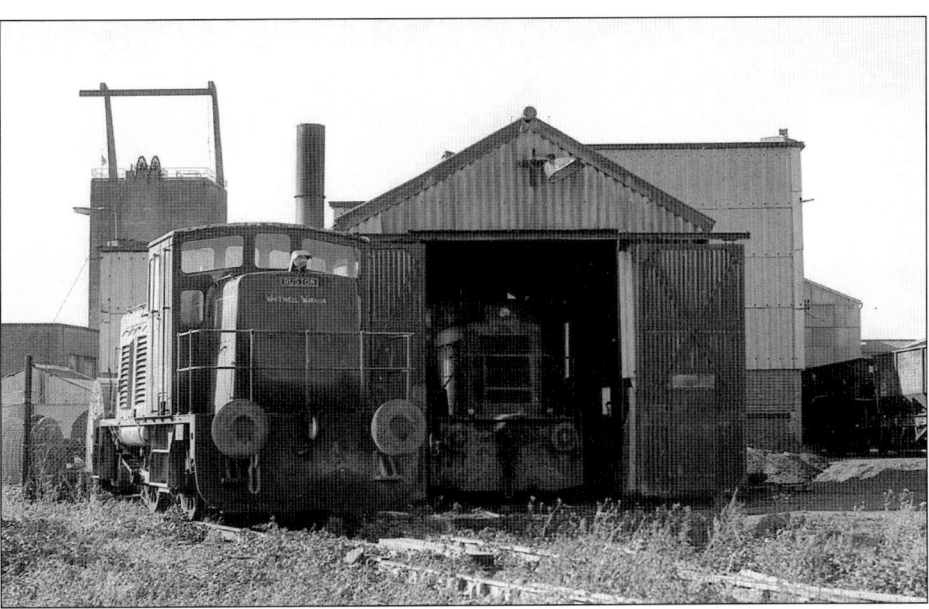

ABOVE: Whitwell also had both colliery and quarry. The wagons in the centre background are in the colliery sidings while the line into the colliery itself runs behind the signal box. The Steetley Doloma(Processing) Ltd. quarry, established in the 1960s, was served by a connection to the right - which descended at 1 in 100 to the quarry sidings - from the main line south of the bridge from which this view was taken. On 28th August 1979 Romanian-built Class 56 No. 56022 brings its train of empty MGR hoppers under the white limestone road overbridge, past the closed station and the signal box. *Adrian Booth.* Of standard Midland Railway design, the 42-lever box dated from 1893, the frame being renewed in 1954. Heavy trains sometimes needed rear-end assistance up the 1 in 110 from here to Elmton & Creswell. The abandoned goods facilities on the left were listed in 1956 as having a 1 1/4-ton permanent crane and equipped to handle all classes of freight. Whitwelll closed to goods on 14th June 1965.

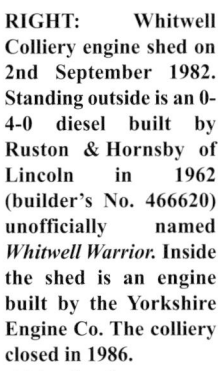

RIGHT: Whitwell Colliery engine shed on 2nd September 1982. Standing outside is an 0-4-0 diesel built by Ruston & Hornsby of Lincoln in 1962 (builder's No. 466620) unofficially named *Whitwell Warrior.* Inside the shed is an engine built by the Yorkshire Engine Co. The colliery closed in 1986.
*Adrian Booth*

ABOVE: A southbound train of empty MGR hopper wagons passes Elmton & Creswell Junction on 24th June 1997 headed by Doncaster-built Class 56 No. 56045. This was the junction with the branch to Seymour Junction and Staveley via Clowne which was still in situ at the time but disused and overgrown as far as Oxcroft beyond which it was still in use. Left of 56045 it can be seen that the points forming the junction have been partly removed. The passenger station was in the course of being rebuilt ready for reopening. The 48-lever signal box is of LMS design built in 1946. *From a Stephen Chapman colour negative*

BELOW: An early 20th century postcard view of Elmton & Creswell station looking north showing the station, the goods depot and the signals for the junction. The stabled coaches on the left and the engine and coaches alongside the goods shed illustrate that some services from Nottingham turned back here. Goods facilities here were listed in 1956 as having a 1½-ton crane and being equipped to handle all classes of freight except livestock. Sidings served Creswell Colliery while there was also Norwood coal siding between here and Langwith. Elmton & Creswell closed to goods traffic on 6th January 1964. *Railway Station Photographs*

**ABOVE:** A modern picture for sure but a scene that is now just a memory. General Motors Type 5 No. 66142 of English Welsh & Scottish Railway hauls a rake of empty MGR hoppers bound for a colliery on the LD&EC through the new Elmton & Creswell station at 13.07 on Tuesday 30th October 2001. The junction to the Staveley branch remains, signalled but partly disconnected, while the line slumbers in vain for a reintroduction of passenger services as an extension to the Robin Hood line project which brought Elmton & Creswell's reopening. *From a Stephen Chapman colour slide*

**BELOW:** Stanier Class 3P 2-6-2T No. 40175 heads a four-coach Worksop-Nottingham train past Langwith Colliery in the 1950s. In the far distance is the bridge carrying the line from the LD&EC Spink Hill line into the colliery. A rapid loading bunker was in operation at Langwith Colliery by 1970 but the pit closed in 1978. *Tom Greaves*

**ABOVE:** The porter at Langwith station waits for any tickets to be collected from alighting passengers as the 5.14pm Nottingham-Worksop arrives behind Stanier 3P 2-6-2T No. 40073 of 16B Kirkby-in-Ashfield shed, at 6.20 on 26th August 1961. *David Holmes*

**BELOW:** Shirebrook Junction on the northern approach to Shirebrook West station - today's Shirebrook station - as 8F 2-8-0 No. 48156 heads coal bound for Kirkby Sidings past the late-Victorian Midland Railway signal box at 2.35pm on 13th October 1962. Curving round to the right is the line to Warsop Junction and the LD&EC while the connection on the left to the wagon works at Langwith Junction has yet to be built. *Robert Anderson*

ABOVE: Shirebrook Junction on Thursday 11th April 2002 showing the steep and sharply curving spur up to W. H. Davies wagon works on the site of Langwith Junction engine shed. Sprinter 156406 is arriving with a Worksop-Nottingham Robin Hood line service. *From a Stephen Chapman colour slide* A short distance beyond the train used to be Welbeck Colliery Branch Junction where the former Midland branch to Welbeck Colliery left the main line from a south-facing connection. The branch was 3 miles 1287 yards long and according to the LMS 1937 Sectional Appendix was a single line worked under One Engine in Steam regulations with a round black staff retained at Shirebrook Junction signal box.

BELOW: Original Great Central O4/1 2-8-0 No. 63597 blasts over Shirebrook Junction and through Shirebrook West station with a trip from the LD&EC to Shirebrook Sidings on Saturday 3rd December 1960. *The late John Beaumont/Robert Anderson collection*

ABOVE: Shirebrook West station at 4.11pm on 13th October 1962 with Fairburn Class 4 2-6-4T No. 42231 on the 3.11pm Nottingham to Worksop. It can be seen that the diesel facilities are already well established in the former goods yard even though the new depot has yet to be built. The fuel tank is in place, the goods shed has been adopted as a makeshift depot and five Brush Type 2 diesels can be seen to be present. *Robert Anderson*

BELOW: Brush Type 4 prototype No. D0280 *Falcon* receives attention outside the former goods shed at Shirebrook depot on 14th October 1962. *Colour-Rail*

Also based at Shirebrook for trials was the Brush 4000hp prototype HS4000 *Kestrel* which on 15th May 1968 began working two 1,600-ton round trips a day to Whitemoor. In August it hauled 2,028 tons from Mansfield Concentration Sidings to Lincoln.

Shirebrook was a small but highly significant diesel depot being crucial in providing the engines and crews that kept the unceasing coal and MGR workings of Sherwood and beyond moving. The first main line diesels, Brush Type 2s(then Class 30) in the area were initially serviced at Langwith Junction steam shed. Diesels are sensitive creatures and the smoke, ash and dust of a steam shed have a detrimental effect on them so it was decided to move to a new, cleaner site. With Shirebrook West goods yard having closed in May 1962, it seemed like a convenient location within easy reach for the Langwith enginemen operating the diesels. The redundant single road goods shed was converted into a temporary diesel maintenance depot and fuelling facilities installed. The modern two-road shed, built to standard Eastern Region design, was completed in June 1965, in time for the closure of Langwith Junction steam shed in February 1966. The shed could house four main line locos and two shunters at a time. At its height it had an establishment of around 70 maintenance staff and 240 train crew.

Shirebrook took the 41J shedcode of Langwith Junction shed and upon the introduction of the TOPS coding system in 1973 became SB. The depot was designed as a servicing base for 30 main line diesel locomotives and 19 of the 350hp diesel shunters but it never had a main line allocation of its own, locomotives being outstationed there, first from Sheffield Darnall, then from Tinsley and finally from Toton. Diesel shunters transferred from Langwith Junction were its only allocation. Over time, main line classes 20, 30, 31, 37, 47, 48, 56 and 58 have operated from Shirebrook besides diesel prototypes *Falcon* and *Kestrel* which were tested on the heavy block coal trains to Whitemoor In the 1980s, the depot became a victim of decline in the coal industry upon which it and its staff depended, its workload reducing rapidly as the pits closed. In February 1991 train crews, along with those from Barrow Hill, were transferred to a brand new signing on point at Worksop where BR was concentrating freight operations. Shirebrook continued purely as a refuelling and examination depot. Eventually time and privatisation caught up with Shirebrook and it was closed by its new owners, EWS, in September 1996.

ABOVE: A Class 20 and a Class 56 "on shed" at Shirebrook in August 1980. *Malcolm Roughley/Stephen Chapman archive*

## LOCOMOTIVES ALLOCATED TO SHIREBROOK
**November 1970: Class 08 0-6-0 diesel:** 3030/325/33/685/701/27/946/4056/66/7/9/70. Total: 12

**In actual fact, Shirebrook had a steam allocation.** In 1968 it was 25-ton steam crane No. 331153 which had a route availability of 7 and was restricted to 30mph, or RA6 restricted to 15mph in an emergency. The lines it covered included: Clipstone-Mansfield Central; Shirebrook North-Fledborough; Worksop East-Kirkby South Junction(exclusive); Langwith Colliery Sidings-Mansfield Town(exclusive); Elmton & Creswell-Oxcroft Colliery No.3; Woodend Junction-Thurcroft and Dinnington collieries; Ollerton-Eakring; and the Bilsthorpe, Blidworth, Rufford, Bevercotes and Mansfield colliery branches. It could also be called to cover serious breakdowns between Oxcroft Colliery No.3 and Foxlow Junction and between Seymour Junction and Glapwell Colliery. The crane was later replaced by tool vans.

**The depot was also home to large independent snowplough** No. DE330966 and medium independent snow plough No. DE330917. These were of the BR standard type mounted on redundant vacuum braked steam locomotive tenders. They could be propelled by any class of locomotive except classes 40, 44, 45 and 46.

ABOVE: A further view of Shirebrook depot in August 1980 showing classes 31, 20, 37 and 56 locomotives and on the right the depot's tool vans and snow plough. On the extreme right is the former Midland branch to Warsop Main Colliery. At weekends, so many locos were stabled at Shirebrook that they had to be parked on the branch as well. *Malcolm Roughley/Stephen Chapman archive*

The Warsop Colliery branch, closed in the 1960s but brought back into use according to a Sectional Appendix supplement issued on 5th April 1980, was shown in the LMS 1937 Sectional Appendix as being single line 550 yards long worked under One Engine in Steam regulations with a round black Staff kept at Shirebrook Station signal box. A branch between Warsop Colliery empty wagon sidings and loaded wagon sidings used a square red Staff retained at the Staveley Coal & Iron Co.'s [then owners of the colliery] shunter's cabin.

BELOW: Looking south from Shirebrook depot with a pair of stabled Class 37s and the 16-lever 1890 Midland Railway Shirebrook Station signal box on the right. The spoil heap of Shirebrook Colliery forms the backdrop. *Malcolm Roughley/Stephen Chapman archive*

**ABOVE:** Superpower for a Worksop-bound train of MGR empties headed by EWS General Motors Type 5s 66232 and 66002 as it passes the now closed Shirebrook depot at 14.41 on Thursday 11th April 2002. It can be seen that the station signal box has gone.
*This and the picture below from colour slides by Stephen Chapman*

**BELOW:** Transition at Shirebrook West. The station is seen with its platforms long since shorn back and the diesel depot disused but when the picture was taken on 24th June 1997 work had begun on rebuilding the station ready for the reintroduction of Nottingham-Worksop passenger trains. Signalling here would also be modernized and these semaphores replaced by a single multiple aspect colour light with a "feather" route indicator for the line to the LD&EC. The station signal box was still in operation at this time.

ABOVE: Romanian-built Class 56 No. 56005 has charge of a fully loaded MGR coal train at Shirebrook Colliery on 28th August 1979. A rapid loading bunker was in use as early as 1968 alongside conventional operations. The colliery closed in May 1993 and the site is now occupied by one of the country's biggest sports goods warehouses. *Adrian Booth*

BELOW: Steam days at Sherwood Colliery in the 1960s with Peckett 0-6-0ST *Sherwood No.4*, builder's No. 1678 of 1927. *Stephen Chapman archive*

ABOVE: A line-up of NCB locos at Sherwood Colliery on 18th September 1979. From left, they are: Roll Royce 4-wheel diesel hydraulic 10194 of 1964, and Thomas Hill 4-wheel diesel hydraulics 170v of 1966 and 247c of 1973. Nos. 10194 and 247c had recently come from Thoresby Colliery which had been converted to MGR operation. Sherwood Colliery, which once employed author and poet D.H.Lawrence's father, closed in 1992. *Adrian Booth*

**ABOVE: Sherwood Colliery Sidings South signal box on 10th July 1982. Sherwood Colliery Sidings marked the boundary between the Eastern and London Midland regions of BR.** *Adrian Booth*

**BELOW: Class 4F 0-6-0 No. 44401 heads the Worksop-Kirkby Sidings pick-up through Mansfield Woodhouse station on 10th October 1964. Mansfield Woodhouse was listed in the 1956 Handbook of Stations as having a 1½-ton permanent crane and able to handle all kinds of goods traffic. The station closed to passengers with effect from 12th October 1964 and to goods from 2nd January 1967. The goods shed, visible above the train, survived demolition and has been incorporated in the new passenger station where it provides cover over a bay platform.** *Tony Cooke/Colour-Rail*

TOP: At Mansfield Town, 24 miles from Shireoaks Junction, original Midland Railway 4F 0-6-0 No. 43953 calls with the Railway Correspondence and Travel Society Midland Requiem railtour of 16th October 1965. From here, the special went to Elmton & Creswell where it took the Clowne line to Seymour Junction and made a return trip to Glapwell Colliery before returning to its starting point in Nuneaton. No. 43953 was one of only three Midland 4Fs remaining in working order by this time and, being presumably judged to be in the better condition of the two, was brought south from Workington specially for this event. The others were 43906 and 43968, both allocated to the much nearer Royston shed, Barnsley. *Stephen Chapman archive*

Mansfield Town goods depot was situated on the east side of the station. It was listed in the 1956 Railway Clearing House Handbook of Stations as equipped to handle all classes of goods but without a permanent crane. The 1938 Handbook listed it as having a 10-ton crane.

Private sidings in and around Mansfield on former LMS lines were: Mansfield and Sutton Cooperative Society; Mansfield Brick and Stone Co.; Mansfield Corporation; Mansfield Standard Sand Co. Ltd. Berry Hill Siding; Mansfield Standard Sand Co. Ltd. Sandhurst Siding; Whiteley Electrical Radio Co.. The 1938 Handbook also listed: Fletcher & Co. (via Mansfield Standard Sand Co. Sandhurst Siding;) Kempson & Co.; Taylor's Kings Mill Siding; Sanderson & Robinson; W. J. F. Sills' Siding between Mansfield and Blidworth; and the Duke of Portland's Bleak Hill Siding.

**The Mansfield-Southwell line** was shown by the 1937 LMS Sectional Appendix as single line worked by Electric Token Block. Token sections were: Mansfield North Jn.-Mansfield Colliery Jn. using a round token with a triangular hole in the centre, and Mansfield Colliery Jn.-Southwell Station using a green key token to Rufford Jn., a blue key token to Blidworth Jn. and a red key token to Farnsfield. A round token was used on the Rufford Colliery branch. The Mansfield Colliery branch was worked as a siding according to One Engine in Steam regulations.

Signal boxes were: Mansfield East Jn.(631yds from North Jn.,) Mansfield Colliery Jn.(1 mile 1575yds.,) Rufford Jn.(1 mile 800yds.,) Blidworth Stn.(1416yds - not a block post,) Blidworth Jn.(775yds.,) Farnsfield Stn.(2 miles 1555yds.,) Kirklington(1mile1571yds.,) Southwell Stn.(2miles 791yds.)

ABOVE. The interior of Mansfield Town station on 6th July 1963 with Stanier Class 4 2-6-4T No. 42587 on the 5.11pm Nottingham-Worksop. Although much of the original station was used in the new 1990s version, it no longer sports an overall roof.
*Tony Cooke/Colour-Rail*

BELOW: Mansfield Town's goods yard pilot, seen at the south end of the station on 21st September 1959, was Johnson Midland Railway 1F 0-6-0T No. 41712. *Tony Cooke/Colour-Rail*

ABOVE: One could easily be deceived by this location. It is Mansfield North Junction which is south of the station. It was so named because it was at the northern point of the triangular junction with the line to Southwell which can be seen in the left foreground. Class 8F 2-8-0 No. 48098 storms south with the 9.30am Creswell Colliery-Kirkby Sidings trip at 10.50 on 19th October 1963. *Robert Anderson*

BOTTOM: Inside the triangle just by South Junction was Mansfield engine shed seen here looking well stocked in early BR days. The engines on show include, from left, Hughes-Fowler "Crab" 2-6-0 No. 42760, a 4F 0-6-0, ex-London, Tilbury & Southend line 4-4-2T No. 41943, and an 8F 2-8-0. *Neville Stead collection/Transport Library.*

Mansfield engine shed was a four road building and was coded 16D in LMS and BR days, changing to 16C in 1955 but closed in April 1960. It boasted quite a large allocation for its size with engines for local passenger and goods services and a selection of 8F 2-8-0s for heavy coal and freight. Among its most celebrated residents were the Whitelegg 4-4-2 tanks released from their native London, Tilbury & Southend line after being replaced by new Stanier 3-cylinder 2-6-4 tanks.

ABOVE: "Tilbury Tank" No. 2098 of the LMS outside the four-road straight shed on 6th June 1936. *Stephen Chapman archive*

**LOCOMOTIVES ALLOCATED TO 16D MANSFIELD IN MAY 1955: 3P 2-6-2T:** 40168/75; **1F 0-6-0T:** 41885; **3P 4-4-2T:** 41940/3/7; **3F 0-6-0:** 43239/431/522/634/711/27; **Midland 4F 0-6-0:** 43874; **LMS 4F 0-6-0:** 44394/415/6; **2MT 2-6-0:** 46501; **8F 2-8-0:** 48001/24/88/119/ 56/272/ 7/405/42/7/621/43/701. **Total: 30**

BELOW: On the Southwell line at Rufford Junction on 9th July 1966 when visited by The Railway Enthusiasts' Club's "The Collier" railtour lead by a Cravens DMU already bearing full yellow ends. The tour of various colliery branches was to have been a Black Five with brake vans until the amount of running round which would be needed was considered. *Chris Gammell/Photos from the Fifties*

LEFT: At work in the Blidworth colliery yard on 16th March 1969 was this 0-4-0ST built by Robert Stephenson & Hawthorns in 1950, builders No. 7644.

The Midland Blidworth Colliery branch was shown in the 1937 LMS Sectional Appendix as single line from Blidworth Jn. worked by One Engine in Steam with a round black staff. The Empty Wagon branch used a triangular red staff to Blidworth Colliery ground frame. A rapid loading bunker was in operation by 1970 though conventional traffic continued as well. Blidworth closed in 1989.
*Horace Gamble/Transport Library*

BELOW: In spite of having lost its regular passenger service as long ago as 1929, the Mansfield-Southwell line was still used for excursions, summer Saturday services and Southwell races specials. In this view 4F 0-6-0 No. 44415 is seen at Farnsfield, 7 3/4 miles from Mansfield, with an eastbound(Up) excursion in 1960. The goods yard on the left was listed in 1956 as having a 1 1/2-ton crane and a vehicle dock. which can just be seen. *Neville Stead collection/ Transport Library*

*Whit. Bank Holiday 27th May 1961 saw three excursions from Blidworth to Cleethorpes hauled by "Crab" 2-6-0s Nos. 42822(of Burton shed,) 42857(of Saltley,) and 42920(of Stoke.)*

**On 27th April 1957 a railtour traversed the Mid-Notts Joint from Farnsfield to Ollerton. In the above view looking towards Farnsfield, the engine, BR Standard Class 2 2-6-2T No. 84006, takes refreshment at Bilsthorpe.** *Stephen Chapman Archive.* **In the view below, taken from the overbridge, gricers leap from the train to inspect Bilsthorpe Colliery sidings. The Staveley Iron Co's. brickworks, which was connected to the colliery by a 3ft gauge line, can be seen on the hillside. Beyond it is Eakring Brail Wood.** *From a Colour-Rail colour slide*

**In the summer 1963 Eastern Region working timetable the one booked train over the Mid-Notts Joint from Ollerton** was a class 8 which ran when required serving the D'Arcy Exploration Co.'s Eakring Sidings, just north of Bilsthorpe: It was booked to leave Ollerton Colliery Jn. at 9.12am and was due at Eakring Sidings by 9.30. On the return it was booked to depart Eakring Sidings at 10.25am, arriving Ollerton Colliery Jn. at 10.37am. London Midland Region coal trains ran between Bilsthorpe Colliery and Farnsfield in the 1960s but at this time LMR local freight trips were planned on a weekly basis by the Divisional Manager, Nottingham. The Working Timetable showed an allowance for trains of 20 minutes from Ollerton to Bilsthorpe and 10 minutes from Bilsthorpe to Farnsfield; 14 minutes was allowed from Farnsfield to Bilsthorpe and 20 minutes from Bilsthorpe to Ollerton.

The Ollerton-Bilsthorpe section was deleted from the Sectional Appendix per the Supplementary Operating Instructions book issued on 27th September 1969, and by this time the entire Southwell line had been abandoned east of Rufford Colliery Junction.

# PLEASLEY AND TEVERSAL

ABOVE: Pleasley West(just Pleasley until 1950,) on the former Midland Railway branch from Pleasley Junction, Mansfield Woodhouse, through D.H. Lawrence country to Teversal. In 1922 it was well served by three Mansfield-Tibshelf-Westhouses & Blackwell-Pye Bridge trains each weekday with four the other way, and two Mansfield-Bolsover-Barrow Hill trains plus one Mansfield-Chesterfield train each way plus extras on Saturdays. But both services were withdrawn and the station closed as early as 28th July 1930. Local goods traffic ended in 1952 but the line continued to serve the collieries in the Teversal area. Pleasley Colliery, which is just out of the picture on the right, closed in 1986 and is being redeveloped as a country park and mining museum. *Railway Station Photographs*

BELOW: The former Midland station at Teversal, sometimes known as Teversal Manor, which was situated just west of the intersection bridge with the GNR. It also closed to passengers in July 1930. Passing through on 12th March 1960 with empty mineral wagons from Tibshelf Sidings to Butcherwood Sidings is 4F 0-6-0 No. 44528. Goods facilities lasted here until 1963. *N. Stead colln./Transport Library*

By the end of the 1960s the Butcherwood area collieries - Sutton, Silverhill, Teversal and Pleasley - were served only from the west with regular trip workings from Tibshelf Sidings on the Erewash Valley line. A dozen class 9 trips were booked from Tibshelf Sidings on Mondays to Fridays in October 1971-April 1972 with 15 returns going mostly to Toton. Tibshelf-Butcherwood Ground Frame trips were timed at Teversal for 01.20-42, 07.11-19, 09.22-30,14.40-48 and 19.17-25. Trips were due at Pleasley East Ground Frame at 12.01, 15.27 and 23.16, the return loaded workings due away at 12.51 and 16.17 for Toton and at 23.10 for Blackwell Sidings.

The Great Northern also had a branch to Teversal from the Leen Valley Extension at Skegby. At Teversal it passed under the Midland branch from Pleasley West Junction to Tibshelf Sidings on the Erewash Valley line before dividing into two routes, one to Teversal Colliery and one to Butcherwood Sidings and Silverhill Colliery. By the end of the 1960s the branch from Skegby had been closed but part of the GN was still used to link Butcherwood Sidings with Silverhill Colliery until its closure in 1992.

ABOVE: This view, taken from the bridge carrying the Tibshelf-Pleasley line, shows the former GN station at Teversal East on the branch to Silverhill Colliery which can be seen in the background. The line curving away to the right goes to Teversal Colliery while coming in beneath the photographer is the line from Skegby. Despite providing the station illustrated, neither the GN or its successors ran an advertised public passenger service. The train pictured in this view is the enthusiasts' special pictured earlier at Bilsthorpe with 2-6-2T No. 84006. Modest goods facilities were provided at Teversal East in the form of the siding seen between the two converging lines. In 1938 they were listed as being able to handle general goods only with no crane. They were withdrawn by BR in 1951.
*Neville Stead collection/Transport Library*

The Midland line from Pleasley Jn. to Pleasley Colliery and Teversal was shown in the LMS 1937 sectional Appendix as worked by Electric Token Block using a round token with a square hole Pleasley Jn.-Pleasley Colliery East, and round token with round hole Pleasley Coll. West-Skegby Jn. (Teversal.)

RIGHT: Out in the cold in Teversal Colliery yard is NCB Barclay 0-6-0ST *Churchill.* Opened in 1867, Teversal Colliery closed in 1980.
*S. Chapman archive*

111

**RUNNING LATE FOR CHESTERFIELD.** This page is devoted to two splendid pictures which arrived too late for inclusion in Railway Memories No.30.
ABOVE: Westhouses-allocated 8F 2-8-0 No. 48507 starts a 1960s Down coal train out of the Up loop at Dronfield where it is viewed from the signal box. Beyond the end of the train can be seen the Unstone branch curving away, which by this time went only as far as Callywhite Public Siding. *Tom Greaves*

BELOW: At the rarely photographed location of Staveley Town between Barrow Hill and Seymour Junction, BR/Sulzer Type 2s Nos. 25020 and 25014 pass the Midland Railway signal box with 8E38, the mid-day Toton to Seymour Junction empties on 4th June 1974. *From a Stephen Chapman archive colour slide*